HEALTH CARE AND

HUMAN VALUES

IDEAS in CONFLICT

Gary E. McCuen

GEM
GARY McCUEN
publications inc.

411Mallalieu Drive
Hudson, Wisconsin 54016
Phone (715) 386-7113

Illustrations & Photo Credits

Carol*Simpson 91, 109, Chuck Asay 48, Common Cause 54, David Seavey 17, Ron Swanson 62, 140, Stayskal 42, 86, Trever 171, Thompson 135, The People 146, U.S. Senate Finance Committee 80, 97, 154, 164, USA Today 104, Web Bryant 12, 37, Richard Wright 26

publications inc.

© 1993 By Gary E. McCuen Publications, Inc.
411 Mallalieu Drive, Hudson, Wisconsin 54016

(715) 386-7113

International Standard Book Number
0-86596-088-7 Printed in the United States of America

CONTENTS

CHAPTER 3 HEALTH CARE OPTIONS: IDEAS IN CONFLICT

CHAPTER 4 RATIONING HEALTH CARE & THE OREGON EXPERIMENT

CHAPTER 5 GLOBAL HEALTH CARE PERSPECTIVES

REASONING SKILL DEVELOPMENT — Interpreting *Editoral Cartoons* 25, Examining *Counterpoints* 71, Reading the *Daily Newspaper* 124, Recognizing *Author's Point of View* 149, What Is *Editorial Bias?* 175

IDEAS
in CONFLICT

This series features ideas in conflict on political, social, and moral issues. It presents counterpoints, debates, opinions, commentary, and analysis for use in libraries and classrooms. Each title in the series uses one or more of the following basic elements:

Introductions that present an issue overview giving historic background and/or a description of the controversy.

Counterpoints and debates carefully chosen from publications, books, and position papers on the political right and left to help librarians and teachers respond to requests that treatment of public issues be fair and balanced.

Symposiums and forums that go beyond debates that can polarize and oversimplify. These present commentary from across the political spectrum that reflect how complex issues attract many shades of opinion.

A *global* emphasis with foreign perspectives and surveys on various moral questions and political issues that will help readers to place subject matter in a less culture-bound and ethnocentric frame of reference. In an ever-shrinking and interdependent world, understanding and cooperation are essential. Many issues are global in nature and can be effectively dealt with only by common efforts and international understanding.

Reasoning skill study guides and discussion activities provide ready-made tools for helping with critical reading and evaluation of content. The guides and activities deal with one or more of the following:

RECOGNIZING AUTHOR'S POINT OF VIEW

INTERPRETING EDITORIAL CARTOONS

VALUES IN CONFLICT

WHAT IS EDITORIAL BIAS?

WHAT IS SEX BIAS?

WHAT IS POLITICAL BIAS?

WHAT IS ETHNOCENTRIC BIAS?

WHAT IS RACE BIAS?

WHAT IS RELIGIOUS BIAS?

*From across **the political spectrum** varied sources are presented for research projects and classroom discussions. Diverse opinions in the series come from magazines, newspapers, syndicated columnists, books, political speeches, foreign nations, and position papers by corporations and nonprofit institutions.*

About the Editor

Gary E. McCuen is an editor and publisher of anthologies for public libraries and curriculum materials for schools. Over the past years his publications have specialized in social, moral and political conflict. They include books, pamphlets, cassettes, tabloids, filmstrips and simulation games, many of them designed from his curriculums during 11 years of teaching junior and senior high school social studies. At present he is the editor and publisher of the *Ideas in Conflict* series and the *Editorial Forum* series.

CHAPTER 1

HEALTH CARE OVERVIEW

1   HEALTH CARE OVERVIEW

THE HEALTH CARE CRISIS

Edward M. Kennedy

Edward M. Kennedy is a U.S. senator from the state of Massachusetts and serves as chairman on the Senate Committee on Labor and Human Resources.

Points to Consider:

1. Who are the un- and under-insured in the U.S.? How many are there?

2. How are senior citizens affected by the health care crisis?

3. Why are rural and trauma hospitals closing down?

4. Why is AIDS a serious burden to the health care system?

Senator Edward M. Kennedy, "The Health Care Crisis: A Report to the American People", Committee on Labor and Human Resources, U.S. Senate, June 1990.

A particularly disturbing aspect of the crisis is its impact on children, who deserve a healthy start in life, but too often fail to receive it.

America faces a health care crisis of unprecedented dimensions.too many Americans are uninsured and underinsured, and the number is growing every year. Too many of the elderly and their families cannot afford essential long-term care. Health care costs are too high and are rising rapidly out of control. Too many health care institutions are facing collapse.

The health care challenge America faces is more serious than at any time since the enactment of Medicare in 1965. No one is immune—young or old, rich or poor, city or farm.

A particularly disturbing aspect of the crisis is its impact on children, who deserve a healthy start in life, but too often fail to receive it. Unless prompt action is taken to address these problems, the future of our Nation's children is a cloudy one, with serious implications for America's future.

The Uninsured and Underinsured

The growing number of the uninsured is unacceptable. In 1979, 29 million Americans were uninsured. Today, the number is 37 million, and it is increasing every year. Sixty million Americans have health insurance that the Department of Health and Human Services found to be inadequate. Altogether, there are almost one hundred million Americans who do not have adequate health insurance protection—more than one-third of the Nation. Half of all Americans contacted by collection agencies every year are in debt because they have medical bills they cannot pay. Even those who are adequately insured today may be at risk tomorrow—if their employer drops coverage, or if the family breadwinner changes jobs or loses a job.

Two-thirds of the uninsured are workers or dependents of workers. They cannot get health insurance at an affordable price, because their employers do not offer it. One-third of the uninsured are unemployed. Lack of adequate insurance can be devastating to families, both in financial terms and in terms of timely access to needed health care.

Long-Term Care

Senior citizens face a crisis, too. They have worked hard all their lives to earn a secure retirement, but their golden years are threatened by the high cost of long-term care. A principal reason why the catastrophic insurance program enacted in 1988 turned into a public policy catastrophe in 1989 is that it failed to provide the protection that senior citizens need most—affordable long-term care.

While senior citizens are especially likely to need long-term care, younger Americans can face the problem, too. The AIDS epidemic, in particular, has exacerbated long-term care needs. Almost three million disabled elderly Americans need home care or nursing home care today. These Americans are unable to perform two or more of the basic activities of daily living without assistance—the ability to bathe, eat, dress, go to the bathroom, or transfer from a bed to a wheelchair.

Of these disabled elderly citizens, 1.3 million reside in nursing homes. Another 1.6 million are struggling to survive in their own homes, in their children's homes, or in other community settings. As many as one million younger Americans are equally disabled. Long-term care is not just a problem for the elderly—it is a major burden for their sons and daughters as well. Few families are prepared—either financially or emotionally—to take the responsibility for meeting the challenges of providing long-term care for parents who need it.

The lack of long-term care is also a serious problem for the health care system. In New York, the shortage of hospital beds is so serious that it is common for patients to stay in emergency rooms for three days before they can be admitted to an inpatient bed. More than 1,000 hospital beds in the city are occupied by people who could be better cared for in nursing homes or through home health care, if such assistance were available.

Rising Costs

The rising cost of health care and the unfair way we finance it are placing a heavy additional burden on the system. The national bill for health care today is $600 billion—more than double what it was in 1980. Health costs are rising twice as fast as wages. Costs for business have become a flash point in labor-management negotiations, where both sides face a difficult choice between reducing health coverage or reducing wages or profits. (In 1992 health care costs went over $800 billion.)

Today, health care costs paid by businesses are 45 percent of corporate operating profits. Small businesses are especially victimized. They pay 20 to 35 percent more than large firms for identical health insurance coverage. American firms struggling to compete in world markets must bear health costs 40 percent

Cartoon by Web Bryant. Copyright 1991, **USA TODAY.** Reprinted with permission.

higher per person than in Canada, 90 percent higher than in West Germany, and more than 100 percent higher than in Japan. Chrysler Corporation faces a built-in cost disadvantage of $300 to $500 per car compared to its foreign competitors because of higher U.S. health care costs.

The high cost of health care to consumers is a constant theme. In St. Louis, managers and union representatives at a Ford Motor Company plant emphasized the competitive difficulties of high health care costs for the company. In Los Angeles, small businessman Jim Krause was unable to obtain health insurance at any price. Edna Dell Weinel, executive director of the Family Care Health Center in Carondelet, Missouri, reported that the center's premiums had jumped 52 percent in one year, and that the center was able to afford policies for its employees only by including a $1,700 deductible for family coverage.

Failing Conditions

The previous factors are contributing to the increasing collapse of health care facilities in all parts of the country. No hospital can survive if it cannot receive adequate revenue to cover its costs. Because of the rising number of the uninsured and inadequately insured patients, the burden of caring for those who cannot pay becomes heavier every year.

The increasing financial pressure on hospitals is reflected in national statistics. One-third of all rural hospitals are operating at a loss; a recent study by the University of Illinois projected that 600 will close in the near future, on top of the 206 that have closed since 1980. Half of all public hospitals are operating at a loss, and the average deficit exceeds $11 million. According to the Joint Commission on Accreditation of Hospitals, 40 percent of the nation's hospitals do not meet health and safety standards, largely because of inadequate financial resources.

In every community that the committee visited, the pressures on key health care institutions were clear. In Los Angeles, 10 out of 18 private trauma care emergency centers have closed their doors, because the affiliated hospitals cannot afford to care for the uninsured patients who enter the hospitals through the emergency center. The result, as Robert Gates, director of Health Services for Los Angeles County, told the committee, is that "Anybody who needs trauma care runs the risk that it is not going to be available."

Drugs and AIDS

In addition to these four basic aspects of the crisis, drug abuse and AIDS are major complicating factors. The drug epidemic is creating a nationwide demand for treatment services and is exacerbating infant mortality. Hospitals in California are spending an additional $500 million to $1 billion a year to care for the stricken infants of drug-dependent mothers. Treatment capacity is sufficient to treat only six percent of addicts at any one time. And intravenous drug abuse is quickly becoming the major transmission route for the AIDS virus.

Spreading Like Cancer

Realistic answers are available to stop this senseless slide and reform our health care system. The question is whether the nation has the political will to do so now, when reasonable remedies can make the difference, or whether it will wait until the current crisis becomes catastrophic and more drastic surgery is required. The cancer analogy is obvious. The longer we wait to deal with the disease, the more the crisis spreads and the more difficult the cure becomes.

HEALTH CARE OVERVIEW

POOR AND MINORITY HEALTH CARE

Association of Minority Health Professions Schools

The Association of Minority Health Professions Schools (AMHPS) is a network of health profession institutions dedicated to improving the health status of minority and disadvantaged persons.

Points to Consider:

1. How does minority health status compare with that of other Americans? Cite several examples.

2. Why is access to health care so closely connected to employment?

3. Why is this so critical to minorities and the poor?

4. How has the number of uninsured minorities increased since 1977? Explain.

Excerpted from testimony by the Association of Minority Health Professions Schools before the Senate Committee on Finance, April 9, 1991.

*Minorities are disproportionately poor and un-
employed, consequently they disproportionately experience the barriers to health care associated with
poverty.*

Blacks and other disadvantaged minorities do not enjoy the
same health status as other Americans. The 1985 Health and
Human Secretary's Task Force Report on Black and Minority
Health demonstrated that there indeed was and is a significant
health status disparity among blacks and other minorities as
compared to the general population of the U.S.

Sobering Facts

Among the more sobering facts revealed by the report were:

- Life expectancy of blacks is nearly six years less than that
  of whites;

- Among blacks, infant mortality occurs at a rate of almost
  20 per 1,000 live births, twice that of whites;

- Blacks suffer disproportionately higher rates of cancer,
  cardio-vascular disease and stroke, chemical dependency,
  diabetes, homicide and accidents; and

Since this historic report by the Secretary in 1985, the health
status gap has widened. The National Center for Health Statistics
recently reported that black life expectancy has decreased from
69.7 in 1984 to 69.2 in 1988. AIDS, which was not even
mentioned in the 1985 report, is now a leading cause of death
and disproportionately affects blacks and other
minorities—minorities who constitute 24 percent of the U.S.
population but 45 percent of our AIDS victims.

The AMHPS (Association of Minority Health Professions Schools)

AMHPS is comprised of eight historically black health
professions schools which have trained 40 percent of the
nation's black physicians, 40 percent of the nation's black
dentists, 50 percent of the nation's black pharmacists, and 75
percent of the nation's black veterinarians.

Each AMHPS institutions has a student body that is
represented by more than 50 minorities. Yet while blacks
constitute 12 percent of the population, only three percent of
physicians are black and only five percent of medical school
graduates (since 1980) have been black. This is important in that

Cartoon by David Seavey. Copyright 1991, USA TODAY. Reprinted with permission

data clearly show that blacks and other minorities are more likely to practice in underserved communities, more likely to care for other minorities and more likely to accept patients who are Medicaid recipients or otherwise poorer than the general population.

AMHPS institutions have been at the vanguard of addressing the enormous need to close the gap in the health status disparity between the minority and majority populations, by increasing the number of minorities in the health professions and by serving the indigent and the underserved.

The Uninsured

There are approximately 37 million Americans who have no health insurance. Millions of disadvantaged Americans are not able to pay for and receive health care.

From 1977 to 1987, the relative increase in the number of persons without insurance was greater among minorities than whites. During that time span, the number of uninsured whites

17

THE GROWING BURDEN

Facing dwindling access to health care and disease prevention information, poor people are experiencing a "growing burden of disease" — and a tendency on the part of society to blame them for their plight, said Dr. Reed Tuckson.

"Sixty thousand black, brown, red and yellow Americans die every year prematurely" because they do not have access to the same resources as "white America", said Tuckson, who is African-American. But "in almost every state the public health system is being dismantled" while new prisons are being built, he said.

Meanwhile, 37 million uninsured Americans find little sympathy for their plight, Tuckson said. Poor, pregnant women often are blamed if they cannot "just say no" to drinking, drugs or cigarettes — even as society withholds access to drug-treatment programs or information about the dangers of smoking that other Americans take for granted, he said.

Demetria Martinez, "Health Care for Poor Is Dwindling, Official says", **National Catholic Reporter**, March 29, 1991

---

increased by about 28 percent while the number of uninsured blacks nearly doubled from four to seven million and the number of uninsured Hispanics increased three-fold from two to six million. Thirty-five percent of Hispanics under age 65 and 26 percent of blacks, were uninsured in 1987 compared to 15 percent of whites. The increase between 1977 and 1987 in the proportion of uninsured Hispanics was five times the increase for whites. For blacks, the increase was twice that for whites. The declining proportion of blacks with health insurance is mainly due to a reduction in private insurance, with public coverage declining.

As the 1985 Secretary's Task Force on Black and Minority Health revealed, "Many. . .minorities tend to rely on Medicaid and charity care for their medical treatment because they have no other sources of care or ways to finance that care. . . ." Further, minorities are disproportionately poor and unemployed, consequently they disproportionately experience the barriers to health care associated with poverty. Under the current system of health care insurance, poor people are too often excluded from the process. Many other barriers exist as a result of poverty which prevent access to health care, including lack of available health care personnel, transportation, and other cultural barriers. Economic and other barriers to the receipt of health care must be eliminated.

Improved access to health care for all Americans must be the primary component of health care reform. In his January 29th State of the Union address, President Bush stated that "good health care is every American's right and every American's responsibility."

3   HEALTH CARE OVERVIEW

HEALTH CARE AND INFANT MORTALITY

The National Commission to Prevent Infant Mortality

The National Commission to Prevent Infant Mortality was chaired by former U.S. Senator Lawton Chiles. After serving in the U.S. Senate, he became Governor of Florida.

Points to Consider:

1. Why is infant mortality so much higher in the U.S.?

2. Why are blacks more prone to infant mortality?

3. Who else is more at risk? Why?

4. What must be done to curb infant mortality in the U.S.?

Excerpted from a report entitled, "Troubling Trends: The Health of America's Next Generation," published by The National Commission to Prevent Infant Mortality, February 1990.

Cities such as Washington, D.C., Detroit and Philadelphia have infant mortality rates which are twice the national average and higher than that of Jamaica or Costa Rica.

After two decades of steady improvement in infant mortality in the United States, the 1980s came as a shock. Progress in reducing the infant mortality rate stalled, resigning the United States to a rank behind nineteen other developed countries in the rate of infant deaths. The gap between white and black infant death rates widened, leaving black infants more than twice as likely to die in infancy as white infants. Progress toward lowering the percentage of infants born at low birthweight stagnated, placing more than one-quarter million infants per year at risk for chronic handicapping conditions. The 1980s also witnessed a growing percentage of women receiving late or no prenatal care, despite the known importance of prenatal care in improving birth outcomes.

Troubling Trends

Compounding these troubling trends, larger societal threats to infant health intensified during the 1980s. A new epidemic of "crack" cocaine use among pregnant women threatened the lives of an estimated 100,000 infants each year. More newborns became infected with the AIDS virus. The effects of poverty, lack of access to prenatal and pediatric care, and exposure to harmful substances such as tobacco and alcohol continued to place pregnant women at risk for poor birth outcomes.

Together, these negative trends have frightening implications for the health of an entire generation of children. Early affronts to fetal growth and development can lead to physical and learning disabilities that cost our nation dearly—in lives lost, increased medical and education costs, and in the long run, a less skilled and less productive workforce. Preventative prenatal and pediatric care can significantly reduce infant death and disability. However, until access is improved and the factors placing pregnant women at risk are reduced and eventually eliminated, the negative maternal and infant health trends of the 1980s will worsen.

Infant Mortality

The infant mortality rate is an important and sensitive gauge of the health and welfare of a population. Of the 3.8 million infants born in the United States in 1987, nearly 39,000 died before reaching age one. With an infant death rate of 10.1 deaths per 1,000 live births in 1987, the U.S. ranked twentieth in infant mortality among the industrialized nations. Since 1981, our country's rate of decline in the infant mortality rate has slowed from 4.7 percent per year in the 1970s to 2.7 percent per year in the 1980s.

But even these numbers, dismal as they are, fail to reflect the true severity of the infant mortality problem. Some regions of the country have become infant mortality "disaster areas" with infant mortality rates much higher than state or national averages and often rivaling the rates in Third World countries. Cities such as Washington, D.C., Detroit and Philadelphia have infant mortality rates which are twice the national average and higher than Jamaica or Costa Rica.

Our persistent high infant death rates demonstrate that past infant mortality reduction efforts have not been sufficient. These current trends provide a strong indicator that infant mortality will worsen in the years ahead, especially as more communities feel the impact of increased poverty among children, drugs, and fewer health care providers serving high-risk families.

Low Birthweight

During the 1970s, the percentage of infants born at low birthweight (under 5-1/2 pounds) declined steadily from eight to seven percent of all births. But throughout the 1980s, the low birthweight rate stagnated at 6.8 percent, with more than one-quarter million low birthweight infants born each year. In 1987, the low birthweight rate showed a disturbing increase to 6.9 percent of all births.

Low birthweight is a major contributor to infant death and disability. Infants born at low birthweight are 40 times more likely to die during their first month of life and two to three times more likely to suffer from chronic handicapping conditions such as blindness, deafness and mental retardation.

Risk factors associated with low birthweight include young maternal age, poverty, low levels of education, high number of previous births, inadequate prenatal care, poor nutrition, smoking, and substance abuse. If the country's infant mortality rate is to decrease substantially in the 1990s, the factors that put mothers at risk of having low birthweight infants must be reduced.

Black-White Infant Mortality Gap

For years, the black infant mortality rate has declined at a slower pace than the white rate, resulting in a widening of the black-white infant mortality "gap". The most recent statistics available indicate that in 1987 the gap between the black and white infant mortality rates was the widest recorded since reporting of these data began in 1940. Black infants are now more than twice as likely to die as white infants.

The gap between the black and white low birthweight rates is also on the rise. In 1987, blacks were nearly three times as likely to be born at very low birthweight (under 3 and 1/4 pounds).

The reasons for the large and growing disparity between the health of black and white infants are not entirely understood. Researchers cite many factors such as access to preventive health services, economic considerations, and unhealthy lifestyles. Closing the unconscionable gap between black and white infant mortality will require a reduction in these risk factors, coupled with action by community leaders and the government.

High-Risk Pregnant Women

Crack use, AIDS, syphilis, and birth to unmarried mothers all increased dramatically during the 1980s. Together these threats have contributed to a "new morbidity" or sickness among American infants.

Recently, the Select Committee on Children, Youth, and Families reported that the incidence of drug-exposed births quadrupled between 1985 and 1989. A 1988 nationwide survey found 11 percent of pregnant women using an illegal drug, with some hospitals reporting rates up to 27 percent. The evidence points to widespread illegal drug use across socioeconomic lines. Crack cocaine use during pregnancy exposes infants to problems ranging from miscarriage to low birthweight, neurobehavorial problems, and congenital malformations.

One-third of infants born to women testing positive for the AIDS virus will show evidence of infection with the virus or die by the age of one. By the end of 1989, there were 1,643 cases of AIDS in children under age five. With the rising incidence of AIDS cases among women of childbearing age, there is little question that pediatric AIDS cases will increase substantially over the next ten years.

In 1988, syphilis cases among infants were at an all-time high, with nearly seven times more cases reported than a decade earlier. Because syphilis in infants can be prevented by detection and treatment early in pregnancy, this increase indicates major gaps in syphilis control and prenatal care. The consequences for infants infected with syphilis include premature birth, low birthweight, and long-term cardiac and neurologic problems. The outlook for the future is poor—the 1989 rate of syphilis infection among women of childbearing age was even higher than in 1988.

The number of infants born to unmarried women in 1987 (933,013) was 40 percent greater than the number reported in 1980 (665,747). The risk of an infant death is nearly twice as high for an unmarried woman as for a married woman. This increased risk is largely attributable to the relative lack of social and financial resources available to unmarried mothers.

Inadequate Prenatal Care

Between 1980 and 1987, the percentage of women obtaining late or no prenatal care increased 26 percent for blacks and 17 percent for whites. In 1987, more than 74,000 pregnant women received no prenatal care at all—amounting to a 50 percent increase over the 1980 rate. These are startling trends in the wrong direction considering the widely known association between prenatal care and healthy births. The most significant barrier to prenatal care is the inability to pay for it.

The Future

The precise impact of these negative trends is unknown. However, it is clear that the steady improvements in infant health that the United States experienced during the 1960s and 1970s stalled in the 1980s and very likely will stagnate in the future unless immediate steps are taken.

The negative maternal and infant health trends of the 1980s cast a shadow on our children's future. This need not be the case. We know that much infant death and disability can be avoided through preventive prenatal and pediatric care. We can no longer rely on advances from expensive, high-tech, neonatal medicine to significantly decrease our infant mortality rate in the future. Rather, we must improve availability and access to preventive health care for pregnant women and infants, and work to change economic and behavioral factors that put pregnant women at risk for poor birth outcomes. Both will help decrease the incidence of low birthweight, the major preventable cause of infant mortality.

INTERPRETING EDITORIAL CARTOONS

This activity may be used as an individualized study guide for students in libraries and resource centers or as a discussion catalyst in small group and classroom discussions.

Although cartoons are usually humorous, the main intent of most political cartoonists is not to entertain. Cartoons express serious social comment about important issues. Using graphic and visual arts, the cartoonist expresses opinions and attitudes. By employing an entertaining and often light-hearted visual format, cartoonists may have as much or more impact on national and world issues as editorial and syndicated columnists.

Points to Consider:

1. Examine the cartoon on the next page.

2. How would you describe the cartoon's message?

3. Try to summarize the message in one to three sentences.

4. Does the cartoon's message support the author's point of view in any of the readings in Chapter One of this publication. If the answer is yes, be specific about which reading or readings and why.

CHAPTER 2

MEDICAL CARE AND SOCIAL JUSTICE

4

MEDICAL CARE AND SOCIAL JUSTICE

EVERYONE HAS A RIGHT TO MEDICAL CARE

Chris Mitchel

Chris Mitchel wrote this article as a research paper for the Network *Board and Staff when he was studying for his Masters Degree in Public Policy at the University of Maryland. It was published in* Network Connections, *a newsletter of* Network, *a national Catholic social justice lobby head-quartered in Washington, D.C.*

Points to Consider:

1. From what tradition does the author draw his conclusions on health care as a human right?

2. What principles are the basis for the Church's teachings on health care?

3. Describe the connection between human dignity and a right to health care.

4. What role should government play?

Excerpted from a research paper by Chris Mitchel, published in **Network Connections,** Spring 1992.

Every person has a basic right to adequate health care. This right flows from the sanctity of human life and the dignity that belongs to all human persons.

As John the Evangelist notes, Jesus came that we might have life and have it to the fullest. During his three years of public ministry, Jesus embarked on a mission of preaching and healing. He brought sight to the blind, hearing to the deaf, and even new life to those who had died. He cured physical ills, but he also calmed people's fears and anxieties. He brought wholeness to those who were experiencing pain and brokenness. Jesus embraced human suffering and transformed it through a healing touch.

Since the time of Jesus' mission the Christian community has sought to continue this ministry of healing. Throughout the history of the Church the health care needs of the people have been an on-going priority. Indeed, through much of the history of medieval Christendom, the Church was the sole provider of organized health care. Religious communities of women, in particular, were in the forefront of health care ministry.

Social Encyclicals

In addition to the ministerial tradition of providing quality health care, the Church has also addressed health care issues through numerous documents and teachings. Especially in recent decades the Church has proclaimed that adequate health care is a fundamental right of the individual; it is not to be a luxury available only to those who can afford to pay. This social teaching on health care is grounded on three primary principles: human dignity, human rights, and social justice.

Human dignity serves as the foundation for all Catholic social teaching. Human beings, created in the divine image, are worthy of the utmost respect. Turning to the "Pastoral Constitution on the Church in the Modern World" of the Second Vatican Council, the Church defines the human person as one "created 'to the image of God', as able to know and love the Creator. . ." As a creature sharing in the divine image, the human person likewise is endowed with the gifts of intellect, love and freedom.

But the dignity of the individual does not consist solely in his or her creation in the likeness of God. Rather, the individual acquires an even greater dignity as one redeemed by Christ. Human nature, by the very fact that it was assumed, not absorbed, in him [Christ], has been raised in us also to a dignity

beyond compare.

Human Dignity

It is this nature which merits for the individual inestimable dignity and worth, and it is this dignity which sets the human person above all other creatures. Upon this radical understanding of the human person, the Church bases its entire social teaching. As individuals sharing in the same common essence, all human persons have the same nature and origin and, being redeemed by Christ, they enjoy the same divine calling and destiny; there is here a basic equality between all and it must be given ever greater recognition.

This teaching—human dignity and equality—has profound implications for human rights in general and rights to health care in particular. John XXIII was one of the first popes to specifically list access to health care as an enumerated human right. In the 1963 encyclical, *Pacem in Terris,* John XXIII taught:

[Women and men have] the right to bodily integrity and to the means necessary for the proper development of life, particularly food, clothing, shelter, medical care, rest, and, finally, the necessary social services. In consequence, [they] have the right to be looked after in the event of ill health. . . .

In positing these rights as inherent to human dignity, John XXIII was not speaking in unrealistic terms. He recognized the practical problems relating to the provision of such services. He was aware of the tremendous expense associated with quality health care; he knew such costs were beyond the means of most individuals. He therefore pointed to the role of governmental bodies in addressing health needs. In *Mater et Magistra* John XXIII wrote: "[these] developments in social living are. . .a cause of growing intervention of the State. . .We might cite as examples such matters as health. . .and the care and rehabilitation of the physically and mentally handicapped." Thus, John XXIII clearly indicates the need for government intervention to ensure adequate access to health care for all persons.

Basic Rights

In "Health and Health Care", the U.S. Catholic bishops reiterate the fundamental premise that health care is a "basic human right which flows from the sanctity of human life". Ultimately, the bishops maintain, concern for one's health lies with the individual and family, but society also has a responsibility for providing adequate health care. All persons, therefore, should have equal access to health care regardless of their socio-economic status or ability to pay. With this as their foundation, the bishops then proceed to outline a series of principles for public policy.

1. Every person has a basic right to adequate health care. This right flows from the sanctity of human life and the dignity that belongs to all human persons, who are made in the image of God. It implies that access to that health care is necessary and suitable for the proper development and maintenance of social or legal status. Special attention should be given to meeting the basic health needs of the poor.

2. Pluralism is an essential characteristic of the health care delivery system of the United States. Any comprehensive health care system that is developed, therefore, should use the cooperative resources of both the public and private sectors, the voluntary, religious and non-profit sectors.

3. The benefits provided in a national health care policy should be sufficient to maintain and promote good health as well as to treat disease and disability. Toward this end, public policy should provide incentives for preventive care, early intervention

WHAT THE CHURCHES SAY

Most mainline American churches take the position that health care is a basic human right that ought to be universally available to everyone. For some of the churches, that position has long been established.

The Union of American Hebrew Congregations similarly believes every person should be "guaranteed essential healthcare coverage."

A National Interreligious Campaign for Universal Health Care is now underway, with 33 faith groups participating. Material prepared for the campaign disclosed four aims:

- *that Americans as a matter of right possess universal access to health care;*

- *that their health care shall be of good quality;*

- *that it shall be comprehensive in scope;*

- *and that such care shall be provided under a system that assures prompt and effective payment to the provider.*

Jim Gittings, "What the Churches Say About National Health Care", **Christianity and Crisis**, Sept. 23, 1991

and alternative delivery systems.

4. Consumers should be allowed a reasonable choice of providers whether they be individual providers, groups, clinics or institutions.

5. Public policy should ensure that uniform standards are part of the health care delivery system.

6. Methods of containing and controlling costs are an essential element of national health policy.

After explaining these fundamental principles, the bishops then go on to make their recommendation that the U.S. create a federally administered national health insurance program: "We call for the development of a national health insurance program. It is the responsibility of the federal government to establish a comprehensive health care system that will ensure a basic level of health care for all Americans." By making this statement the bishops seek to give weight to the argument in support of national health insurance, especially as it impacts on the poor.

Concern to All

CHA (Catholic Health Association) views the health care needs of the nation as a concern for all segments of society—the individual, the family, the churches, the private sector, the federal and state governments, etc. To meet the health needs of all Americans a coordinated effort from all these parties is necessary.

MEDICAL CARE AND
SOCIAL JUSTICE

MEDICAL CARE IS NOT A
HUMAN RIGHT

Stephen Chapman

Stephen Chapman's editorials on public issues are nationally syndicated. He is a well known conservative writer.

Points to Consider:

1. Why does the author disagree with Harris Wofford?

2. Why don't working Americans have a right to medical care?

3. How is the First Amendment referred to in this context?

4. Do citizens have a right to any kind of health care?

Excerpted from articles by Stephen Chapman appearing in the **Conservative Chronicle** entitled "Prescribing More Government Isn't a Cure", December 11, 1991, and "Do Americans Have a Right to Medical Care?", December 18, 1991. By permission of Stephen Chapman and Creators Syndicate.

***A right to medical care . . .lets you infringe on the
liberty and property of others.***

When an unknown named Harris Wofford upset former U.S.
Attorney General Dick Thornburgh in the U.S. Senate race in
Pennsylvania, experts ascribed the victory largely to Wofford's
advocacy of national health insurance, and the success of that
position to one particularly deft commercial. Standing in a
hospital, the candidate said that the Constitution guarantees
criminals the right to a lawyer. "If criminals have the right to a
lawyer," Wofford continued, "I think working Americans have the
right to a doctor."

This is a *non sequitur* (an illogical statement) , but an
exceedingly clever one. It makes criminals look privileged and
honest people look deprived, while suggesting that our health
care problems can be remedied by simply recognizing that
medical treatment is a right.

No Logic

But there is no logic to this reasoning. You could use
Wofford's formulation to justify almost anything. If criminals have
the right to a lawyer, working Americans have the right to (take
your pick) affordable child care, a college education, safe
streets, clean air, paid parental leave, an honest Congress—the
list is endless, and senseless. It's about as illuminating as the
old line that "if we can put a man on the moon, we should be
able to. . . ."

Criminal suspects—not criminals, as Wofford put it—have the
right to a lawyer only because of the unique circumstances in
which they find themselves—in the custody of the state,
deprived of their normal liberty, perhaps prevented from earning
a living, facing imprisonment or execution.

The government has a duty to furnish a lawyer to poor
defendants (not all defendants) because the government has put
them in jeopardy. Asked why, if criminals have a right to a
lawyer, working Americans don't have a right to a doctor, Kent
law professor Randy Barnett replies, "Because the government
didn't make you sick." If the government did cause your illness,
it would be obligated to compensate you.

We provide criminal suspects with lawyers mainly to assure
that they aren't put in prison unjustly. Working Americans in
need of a doctor are in no such danger. But it's tempting to say
that because they want and need medical care, they have a

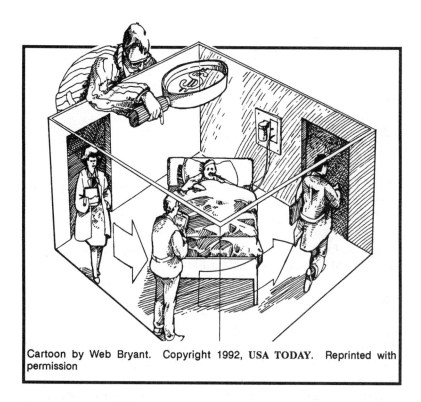

Cartoon by Web Bryant. Copyright 1992, USA TODAY. Reprinted with permission

right to it.

This is an error. One reason is that it perverts the understanding of rights enshrined in the Constitution, which are summarized as "life, liberty and property". This view essentially means the government is obligated not to do certain things to you, not that it is obligated to do anything for you. The First Amendment guarantee to freedom of the press means it may not stop you from writing and publishing whatever you want, not that it must give you a printing press.

A Blank Check

A right to medical care, on the other hand, means the government has to provide you with things that are far more expensive than a printing press. It is a blank check drawn on the bank accounts of the taxpayers at large. Instead of protecting your liberty and property, as rights are meant to do, this one lets you infringe on the liberty and property of others.

If you exercise your right to press freedom, you impose no burden on anyone who doesn't want to pay to read your newspaper. If you exercise your right to medical care, you may stick your neighbors with hundreds of thousands of dollars in bills they have to cover out of their own earnings.

It may be argued that medical care is a right because it is a matter of life and death. Most medical care isn't about any such thing. People may be uncomfortable or unhappy if they can't get treated for slipped discs, ear infections, skin rashes, enlarged prostates or arthritic knees. But they won't die.

When it comes to true emergencies, we as a society do try to assure that no one goes without medical services, which is why we have public hospitals, as well as Medicaid and Medicare. But trying to assure that no one dies for lack of treatment is a long way from conferring a fundamental right to medical care.

It could be said that, in practice, we do recognize some sort of right to food, housing and other necessities, which is why we have welfare programs. The right being talked about here, however, is a far more extreme concept.

It means not that people have a right to a certain minimum level of health care at public expense if they can't afford it, but that they have a right to the best treatment they can find at public expense even if they can afford it. Not even the most radical advocate for the homeless argues that they have the right to the best housing available, or that the government has a duty to provide exactly the same housing, free, to everyone.

Something for Nothing

Thanks to Medicare, Medicaid, public hospitals, tax-subsidized employee health insurance and other government programs, Americans have gotten the idea that every person has a right to the best care at someone else's expense. If the medical care is a right, it's deeply unjust to demand any financial sacrifice from its recipients. Here, the entitlement ethic has spread far and wide. Everyone wants to live at the expense of everyone else.

This desire is encouraged by the belief that people elsewhere have invented a way to do just that. Canada allows patients to choose their private doctors, but virtually all bills are paid, and all fees set, by the government. Its approach has reputedly given Canada both lower medical costs and better health than the United States. Canadians, unlike Americans, are also happy with their system. But it's easy to see why it enjoys such popularity: it's practically free. The U.S. Postal Service may not work very well, but if you could send anything from a first-class letter to a truckload of furniture at no cost, you'd be content with it.

Neither mail nor medicine can really be delivered for free—citizens pay directly in fees or indirectly in taxes. But by

CIVIL RIGHTS

Health insurance covers many "volitional illnesses", damage people do to themselves by behavior they should know is harmful. Few would argue that someone whose hobby is Russian roulette has a right, let alone "civil right" to insurance against the risk. Certain illnesses more closely resemble injuries resulting from Russian roulette than illnesses deriving from the unavoidable lottery of life — illnesses unrelated to risky habits.

Such behavior includes smoking, drinking excessively, exercising too little, eating unwisely, abusing drugs, and driving recklessly. Civil rights, properly understood, are those central to civic life. They do not include the right to insurance coverage for all of one's behaviorally based ailments.

George F. Will, "Health Insurance Becomes 'Civil Rights' Issue", **Conservative Chronicle**, Aug. 25, 1988

separating the payment from the service, the government allows its constituents to think they're getting something for nothing.

Government Interference

Letting Washington assume all responsibility for paying for every citizen's medical care is supposed to save us all huge sums in administrative costs by substituting a single payer for the hundreds that exist now. If you believe this, you'll believe that cars would be cheaper if only one manufacturer were allowed to sell them.

That's no stranger than thinking the demand for medical care won't soar once patients are freed from the burden of payment. If the government assured every American a new car every five years at public expense, the nation would soon find itself spending a lot more on automobiles.

By spending more on medical care, the government has caused us all to get less medical care. It has also rapidly driven up the cost of treatment, making it harder for anyone but the government to afford. Most proposed remedies for our health care problems are complicated, imperfect and frustrating.

6 MEDICAL CARE AND SOCIAL JUSTICE

A CORRUPTED HEALTH CARE SYSTEM

Matthew Dumont

Matthew Dumont, a Boston physician who has written a book on the psychiatric treatment of the poor, wrote this article for Newsday.

Points to Consider:

1. What was Hippocrates' approach to medical ethics?

2. How have market values corrupted the medical profession?

3. How do doctors "cash in" on the capitalist market system?

4. Who monopolizes the free-market system? How?

Matthew Dumont, "Doctors Now Are as Ready to Fill Graves as Cradles", Minneapolis **Star-Tribune**, Jan.13, 1992.

What looks like a free-market affair is actually a monopolized and artificially inflated one. While obstetricians are off fertilizing test tubes, millions of low-income women are not getting the most basic prenatal care.

Medical historians will remember the first half of this century as the one that fell asleep under the kind eyes and gentle hands of Dr. Kildare and woke up manacled under Dr. Mengele. Now, another half-century after the Nuremberg trials demonstrated what doctors are capable of, a new medical persona has taken hold of the culture's pulse. Reflecting, as always, the values of the rest of society, the practice of medicine has become technologically expert, dominated by a business mentality and ethically bankrupt.

Hippocrates taught that one should be a philosopher before becoming a physician. For centuries since, despite their lethal blundering and pompous stupidity, the phrase "doctor's orders" meant something, for doctors were expected to be dedicated to their patients, wise, prudent, moral and guided by an almost sacred code of ethics that took precedence over any other inclination, including, at times, the patient's own.

The Market

Medicine, however, is now ready to provide any cradle-to-grave service to the highest bidder, and the only guide seems to be the "invisible hand" of the market. The art of formal, official and legal murder is only one of the more eye-catching commodities in the medical mall. Doctors have always killed their patients by mistake or informal restraint of aggressive treatment for someone dying in agony. But now, with Dr. Jack Kevorkian's handy machine and a "Whose life is it anyway?" populism, doctor-assisted death may become as routine as the death penalty. In some "progressive" states they are the same thing. The brutality of the gas chamber and electric chair is being replaced by lethal injections administered by physicians.

The state of Massachusetts, which only recently apologized for the executions of Sacco and Vanzetti, is being induced by its governor to institute a doctor-mediated death penalty. A colleague, recently unemployed because of the same governor's cutbacks in health services, shrugged and said, "A job's a job."

The market, like nature, abhors a vacuum, and doctors are showing themselves as ready to fill graves as cradles on

"WE DID IT! FOUND A CURE FOR THOSE POOR HELPLESS SOULS LIVING IN TORMENTING AGONY WITHOUT HOPE...IF, OF COURSE, THEY CAN AFFORD IT!"

demand.

Hopeful consumers of artificial insemination, *in vitro* fertilization or the other models of unnatural baby-making are often a little shocked at the entrepreneurial atmosphere in the clinics they visit. Even car dealers do not ask for your credit card number before saying, "Good morning". And no automobile hype can match the advertised claims of infertility centers, which count a missed period a "success".

With infertility, Caesarean-sections and low birth weight now commonplace, the medical domination of what used to be a natural process has become total and complete. Almost every hospital has its own neonatal intensive-care unit designed to keep alive a fetus weighing as little as a pound. The rate of handicaps among the survivors may be as high as 60 percent, but if you want a baby against the odds, and have the money, the doctors are ready and waiting.

So are the providers of sperm for artificial insemination. For an additional fee, the sperm may even be gleaned from a bevy of Nobel laureates and other aging geniuses on the assumption that their intelligence rather than their looks will be passed on to the lucky egg.

As supplies are limited, you may not be able to order a

genius, but it is certainly possible to express a sexual preference. In India, upper-class women are routinely obtaining amniocenteses and choosing to abort female fetuses. Misogyny may not be so straightforward in America, but a preference for male children still predominates. On the other hand, there are reports that some lesbians have chosen to abort their male fetuses. The thing about medical technology on the market is that when something *can* be done, you can expect that it *will* be done. Before long, it will seem that it *should* be done.

The medical profession is prepared to cash in at the other end of the life cycle. While not yet a mail-order item, you can, at a price, arrange for the freeze-drying of your not quite dead body, to be thawed out in some utopian time when you will be welcomed back to life by a future generation applauding your reentry with their little cockroach tentacles.

More mundane is the transplant, or artificial-organ variety of immortality, with doctors as spare-part suppliers. We have already seen the bodies of poor women used as plantations to grow babies for the rich. One can imagine a time when the bodies of their babies are routinely farmed for their organs.

The spirit of capitalism is built on appetite, and not since cannibalism was common has there been such a lust for human parts. There seems to be no currently legal way for the supply of donors' organs to keep pace with demand. A recent American Medical Association (AMA) publication survey of 100 transplant physicians found that 78 percent of them, impatient with the shortage of organs, are in support of "presumed consent." This means that a dead biker's kidneys can be taken at will unless there is definite proof that he did not want them donated.

On a happier note, more and more members of the profession are signing aboard the Love Boat. Since Aphrodite's profession was just one of several, along with medicine, granted divine status by the ancient Greeks, it is only reasonable to find medicine and beauty in bed together at the market. Ads for plastic surgeons can be found in fashion magazines, and for a fraction of their fortunes, anyone can have Elizabeth Taylor's eyes or Paul Newman's chin.

Beauty has always been stalked by racism, so it is no surprise that in overdeveloped Japan, Western eyes can be purchased to go with the diamonds and whiskey now thought to make life worthwhile. Elsewhere, lips are being thickened or thinned, cheeks and buttocks tucked and breasts made bigger or smaller.

There are more direct routes to pleasure, and free-market medicine is always available to pursue them, relying on the doctor as drug pusher. Sleep, euphoria, pain relief, stimulation and tranquility are available in a variety of drug forms, with the distinction between the legal and illegal ones as thin as a prescription blank. A couple of journalists in a Northeast city reported some years ago that 40 percent of the doctors they offered to pay in cash were ready to provide them a prescription for a requested controlled substance without bothering to take a history or perform a physical examination. The rich and powerful have always had access to high-priced physicians.

Ethics

Where is ethics in all this? Ethical considerations have a way of being ignored when market forces are compelling. The quantum leaps of medical technology are so rapid that their consequences cannot be known.

Ethics do not come fully formed from the head of "ethicists". They require a more patient and retrospective analysis of social costs and benefits than our future-oriented, profit-seeking society likes to offer. In their rush to market, doctors have forgotten even the most basic and enduring of ethical guidelines: *primum non nocere* — above all, do no harm.

What looks like a free-market affair, however, is actually a monopolized and artificially inflated one. Considering the enormous amount of public money going into the training and regulation of physicians, everyone is paying for the administration of an exotic commodity to the narcissistic few. And the siphoning off of so much medical attention means, as it always does, the further deprivation of the poor. The emergency wards of the major cities in at least 41 states have become disaster zones choked with seriously ill patients waiting days for a bed. And while obstetricians are off fertilizing test tubes, millions of low-income women are not getting the most basic prenatal care. In some areas an obstetrician who will accept a patient on Medicaid cannot be found.

Before America embarks on a national health program, there will have to be a full and open debate about what our priorities in health are. We may decide that we need more generalists in medicine and fewer highly paid specialists who cannot think of an entire patient, to say nothing of the whole community. Health care, like a clean environment, is a responsibility to all and not a matter of the capricious whims of individuals who want what they want when they want it.

MEDICAL CARE AND
SOCIAL JUSTICE

THE BEST MEDICAL CARE IN
THE WORLD

Floyd D. Loop, M.D.

Floyd D. Loop is a medical doctor and Chairman of the Board of Governors and CEO of the Cleveland Clinic.

Points to Consider:

1. How have the advances in medicine and surgery been forgotten?

2. Why does the U.S. medical profession remain the best in the world?

3. Why are physicians not to blame for problems in health care?

4. What does the author see as a solution to our health care crisis?

Floyd D. Loop, M.D., "Modern Medicine", **Vital Speeches of the Day**, December 13, 1991.

In comparing developed countries, the U.S. has the best medicine in the world.

Why are people so unhappy with health care? We have state-of-the-art, innovative, and technologically advanced medicine in the United States. Yet we are dissatisfied. What are the problems? Some are medical; more are societal: 1) 32 million people are uninsured. 2) Drug abuse, poverty, and teenage pregnancy are unrelenting despite increasingly costly public health efforts. 3) The elderly are growing in numbers, living longer, and incurring more cost. 4) The financing of health care is a crazy quilt that engenders high administrative costs. 5) There are too many specialists and too few primary care physicians. 6.) There is the question of quality and effectiveness of some treatments.

The biggest problem involves the growing number of uninsured, who make up about 13 percent of our population or 32 million people. And this group has grown in the past decade because the United States is changing from a manufacturing to a largely service economy, where businesses are generally smaller.

The Villains?

What would the public prefer? The polls show that the public wants total freedom of access, and for employers to pay everything. That is the expectation of our American civilization. Two-thirds of Americans surveyed believe that we spend too little on health care and believe that 20 percent of the gross national product spent on health is not too much. According to some polls, the respondents favor some kind of universal health system, but only a small minority would be willing to contribute more than two hundred dollars a year per person for it. This is the same public that spends 100 billion dollars a year on alcohol and cigarettes.

The villains are said to be overuse of technology and the high price of care. Somehow, amidst this rancor and discontent, the advances of medicine and surgery have been forgotten. I assure you those days are gone when half the patients were cured by putting them to bed, and the other half by getting them up. Would you prefer an era when there were no antibiotics, orthopedic reconstructions, organ transplants, or coronary care units? In the 1950s there were more people in the hospital for hemorrhoids than there were for heart disease. More people underwent hernia repair than were hospitalized for cancer. This

Cartoon by Chuck Asay, **Colorado Springs Gazette Telegraph.**

same public must not be aware that mortality from heart disease has dropped more than 30 percent in the past 30 years (30 percent reduction from heart disease and 50 percent from stroke). Except for lung cancer, some of which is self-inflicted, cancer deaths have also declined significantly in recent years. Science and medicine have added 26 years to our lifespan in the 20th century alone.

The Best

We take very good care of the elderly in this country, probably better than anywhere in the world. Seventy-one percent of entitlements go to the elderly. As the result of an extended aging process, we now spend about as much on elderly health care as a person receives in his lifetime from Social Security. Not including administrative costs, in 1990 the United States spent 144 billion dollars on Medicare and Medicaid, or 12 percent of the federal budget.

If one measures economy by total domestic output per person, the United States has the most productive economy in the world. We also devote more dollars to health care per person than any other country. At the end of the 1980s, our health care consumed 11 percent of the gross domestic product, compared with 9 percent for Sweden, Canada, and France, 8 percent for West Germany, 7 percent for Japan, and 6 percent for the U.K.

How do other nations do it? Look at Canada. They spend less and they do it by four methods: rationing, regulating medical fees, limiting access to technology, and controlling growth of technology.

In hospitalization, we compare favorably to all countries. Hospitalization rates in the U.S. are among the lowest in the world. Our length of hospital stay averages seven days and is below that of any industrialized country. There is a tremendous shift away from hospital care to home care in this country. Most of the other countries have lengths of hospitalization between 12 and 17 days.

Our health care is sometimes cited as inadequate because we are 18th in the world in infant mortality, which to me says more about our society than about health care. We have a one percent infant mortality rate compared to 0.5 percent in Japan. The rest of the developed nations are somewhere in between. None of them have our problems with drugs, teenage pregnancy, crack babies, and homicides. But when you look at U.S. citizens who reaches 65, they can expect to live as long or longer than older people in any of the comparative countries.

Physicians

Let's step back from medicine a minute and look at the individual physician. Did doctors cause all these problems? I don't think so. They are pushed along by scientific advances and by the social pressures of change. Physicians' fees account for only 20 percent of the health care cost in this country. Strict regulation of physicians' fees is a one-time gain and would affect only a small amount of the overall cost of medicine. Cost is more related to technological advances, inflation, personnel, the aging society, and the legitimate demands from patients for advanced treatment.

The best investment you can make in life, apart from your family, is to find a talented and experienced physician who can guide you carefully and confidently through the maze of technology and treatments.

Solutions

Assuming that we can build discipline into the system, I favor combining public and private spending to care for the underprivileged. There is no way around more taxes. Sin and disease taxes, such as alcohol and tobacco, should be the first line of revenue enhancement. And I would also add a tax on lotteries. This is going to be better than trying to reform health care through one of the proposed universal health plans.

I am not persuaded that we need more physicians. We need less paperwork and more attention to quality of care. The Institute of Medicine reports that a small number of physicians account for a large number of quality problems. Every state legislature should be responsible for passing a tough medical practice act. Those who do odious deeds should be thrown out of medicine.

People don't come here anymore to see how we build TVs or automobiles, but they still come to America for higher education and for health care. In comparing developed countries, the U.S. has the best medicine in the world; our medical progress is limitless, but so is the potential for economic expansion. While our medical care system works well for the great majority of Americans, the growing number of uninsured people must be provided for. Medical indigence is more of a societal than a medical problem.

We have molded the character of our American health care system to the demands of our American way of life. We encourage and support the development of technologic advances and we demand access to these advances as a

Constitutional right. The more convenience and sophistication that is desired by the consumer, the more it will cost. We must recognize that all costs of medicine are eventually paid for by people.

I have seen the alternatives offered by other countries. In my surgical career, I have travelled extensively and performed heart surgery in 10 countries around the world. My optimism and idealism about value in American medicine is based on the fact that I am associated with a superb health care model and I see the good parts of our system working every day.

8

MEDICAL CARE AND
SOCIAL JUSTICE

THE MEDICAL INDUSTRY
BLOCKS REFORM

Vicki Kemper and Viveca Novak

Vicki Kemper is associate editor and Viveca Novak is a senior staff writer for Common Cause Magazine.

Points to Consider:

1. Who are the medical industry's PACs (Political Action Committees) and why do they give money to lawmakers?

2. Who are the top recipients of PAC money?

3. Why has the AMA resisted health care reform?

4. How are doctors and insurance companies involved?

Vicki Kemper and Viveca Novak, "What's Blocking Health Care Reforms?", **Common Cause Magazine,** January/February/March 1992.

The real culprit may be the medical industry money that helps keep politicians in office.

Reform proposals—calling for everything from minor treatment to major surgery—have been pouring out of medical associations, insurance companies, labor unions, businesses, grassroots organizations and *ad hoc* coalitions. Even the American Medical Association (AMA), which has used money and hardball politics to fight government-sponsored health care programs since the early part of this century, has its own limited prescription for universal coverage. Dozens of reform bills are pending in Congress.

But whether electioneering and political rhetoric will translate into concrete action is another question. Given the obvious need for change, who or what is standing in the way? President George Bush and his advisers have rejected calls for a systemic overhaul and instead suggested only limited reforms, including an emphasis on "healthier lifestyles".

Congress has not done much better. Many Democrats want comprehensive reform but can't agree on what kind. A Senate Republican task force, after months of caucusing, produced a proposal that leaves the current system essentially intact, and a group of House Republicans met weekly for more than six months without introducing a bill.

Meanwhile, doctors blame lawyers and the government for the current mess. Health care purchasers point to insurance companies that cover only the healthy, while insurers single out greedy doctors and hospitals and unrealistic consumers.

For all this finger-pointing, few in Washington are willing to blame what may be the biggest culprit of all: the political influence of special interest groups with a vested interest in the *status quo*. The same insurance companies, doctors, hospitals and drug manufacturers that live off the $700 billion-a-year health care industry are battling comprehensive reform on Capitol Hill and at the White House.

PACs (Political Action Committees)

Throwing money at the process are more than 200 political action committees (PACs)—representing everything from the legendary AMA to the obscure Philippine Physicians in America. Together these medical, pharmaceutical and insurance industry PACs contributed more than $60 million to congressional candidates between 1980 and the first half of 1991. PAC

TOP 25 RECIPIENTS OF MEDICAL INDUSTRY PAC CONTRIBUTIONS

(JANUARY 1, 1981 - JUNE 30, 1991)

	Medical-Industry PAC Contributions
1. Representative Pete Stark (D-CA)	$497,250
2. Senator David Durenberger (R-MN)	496,462
3. Senator Lloyd Bentsen (D-TX)	413,050
4. Senator Max Baucus (D-MT)	374,165
5. Representative Henry Waxman (D-CA)	360,805
6. Representative Charles Rangel (D-NY)	356,712
7. Representative Richard Gephardt (D-MO)	356,525
8. Senator Orrin Hatch (R-UT)	347,629
9. Senator Bill Bradley (D-NJ)	343,749
10. Senator Dan Coats (R-IN)	320,418
11. Representative Robert Matsui (D-CA)	307,750
12. Senator Robert Dole (R-KS)	303,073
13. Representative Robert Michel (R-IL)	295,850
14. Senator John Rockefeller (D-WV)	293,072
15. Senator Thomas Daschle (D-SD)	289,083
16. Senator John Chafee (R-RI)	285,408
17. Senator Phil Gramm (R-TX)	283,837
18. Senator Steve Symms (R-ID)	279,283
19. Senator Tom Harkin (D-IA)	270,404
20. Representative Beryl Anthony (D-AR)	269,900
21. Representative Byron Dorgan (D-ND)	254,196
22. Senator John Danforth (R-MO)	250,635
23. Representative Norman Lent (R-NY)	250,130
24. Senator Arlen Specter (R-PA)	245,361
25. Senator Richard Shelby (D-AL)	244,682

Source: **Common Cause**

contributions from the health care industry have increased far more than gifts from most other special interests: 140 percent over the last decade, compared with 90 percent for all PACs.

Almost half the contributions from the health industry to current members of Congress came from physicians, dentists, nurses and other health professionals; health insurance companies contributed nearly one-third of the total; and the remainder came from pharmaceutical companies, hospitals, nursing homes and other health care providers. The money was carefully targeted: more than $18 million—or 42 percent—of the contributions went to members of the four congressional committees that have jurisdiction over health-related legislation.

Twelve of the 21 senators who received more than $200,000 from medical industry PACs serve on the Finance Committee, which has jurisdiction over Medicare and other health-related matters, as well as tax policy. All of the top 25 House recipients of medical industry PAC money serve in House leadership positions or on the key Ways and Means or Energy and Commerce committees.

All that medical industry money hasn't bought better health care—but that's not what it's for. What it has bought is access in Washington for physicians, hospitals and insurance and pharmaceutical interests, along with inaction on the issue of health care reform.

"We spend our money on those members. . .most interested in maintaining the current system," says Tom Goodwin, public affairs director of the Federation of American Health Systems. The federation, which represents some 1,400 for-profit hospitals, has contributed $934,709 to congressional campaigns since 1980, making it the 11th-biggest giver among health-related PACs.

The stream of health-related PAC money into Washington has swelled at a time when U.S. spending on health care has shot past other economic indicators. Health care spending now accounts for 13 percent of the country's GNP—the highest proportion in the world—and it will consume 37 percent by the year 2030 if costs continue to increase at their current rate, according to Richard Darman, director of the Office of Management and Budget.

Washington has done little over the years to contain health care costs—at least in part, many believe, because of the PAC contributions that have bought political access for physicians, hospitals and insurance and pharmaceutical firms. "The monied interests have caused gridlock," says Dr. Robert Berenson, a Washington, D.C., physician who served on President Jimmy Carter's domestic policy staff.

Insurance companies represent one huge obstacle. "They are actually against doing anything, because they realize that any kind of reform is going to involve some federal regulation of the insurance industry," says Robert Blendon, chair of the Department of Health Policy And Management at the Harvard University School of Public Health.

Most Americans dislike insurance companies, but few politicians are willing to take on the industry. Insurance PACs have contributed $19 million to congressional candidates since 1980, and seven of the top 20 medical industry PACs are affiliated with insurance companies or associations.

House Calls

Health care reform has never fared well politically in the United States, and for most of the 20th century there has been one enduring reason: the intractable opposition of the AMA.

AMA resistance persuaded Franklin Roosevelt to leave health care out of the New Deal, and when President Harry Truman promoted a plan for national health insurance, AMA members wrote him angry letters on pink paper labeling the plan a "communist plot". The organization spent a phenomenal $1.3 million in nine months — $7.1 million in today's dollars — to defeat Truman's plan.

John Kennedy made federally guaranteed health care for older Americans a key element of his 1960 presidential campaign platform. But even Medicare, a boon for tens of millions of the elderly — not to mention doctors and hospitals — was enacted over the strident opposition of the AMA.

The passage of Medicare and Medicaid were the last significant government actions to help large numbers of

Americans gain access to affordable health care. In the 1970s, politics and interest-group opposition defeated numerous initiatives for further reform, and for the Reagan administration, health care reform wasn't even a blip on the screen.

Meanwhile, the AMA and its state affiliate PACs have contributed more than $11.9 million to congressional campaigns since 1980 — along with some $3 million "independent expenditures" made on behalf of certain candidates. That's more than double the amount of contributions made by any other health-related PAC.

Still, times have changed even for the powerful, anti-government AMA. The group issued its own health care reform proposal in March 1990. "The doctors have been very smart on this," says Harvard's Blendon. "After 50 years of saying 'do nothing', they come out and say they're for universal coverage." By plunging into the debate with its own proposal, the AMA has "positioned itself to play a big role," he adds.

But there's a catch: The AMA wants to make sure Congress protects doctors from malpractice suits and doesn't hit them with cost controls, and its proposal reflects those concerns. Likewise, reform proposals pushed by insurance companies, hospitals, drug manufacturers and other interest groups emphasize their varying and self-serving priorities.

No Easy Cure

Of course, health care reform won't come cheap. Even the limited proposals carry estimated price tags of $10 billion over five years. For the more sweeping reform proposals, there are widely varying cost estimates — and while sponsors prescribe different methods of paying for universal coverage, almost all would require tax hikes of some kind.

A key sticking point is how to control health care costs. Limited reform proposals would merely control access to health care services. Naturally, doctors and hospital administrators strongly oppose efforts to regulate their fees.

Bitter Medicine

Significant movement on the issue would require overcoming the insurance companies and small businesses that oppose all but the mildest reform proposals. A single-payer system would do away with the need for most private health insurance, and insurance executives worry that a pay-or-play system would give employers more incentive to pay into the public program than to provide their employees with private insurance. "We oppose that strenuously, and are working to see that it is not enacted," says David Hebert of the National Association of Life Underwriters.

The wealth and power of the insurance industry are hard to overstate. "The health insurance industry. . .has tons of money and they love to spend it to get their way on Capitol Hill," says Public Citizen spokesperson Robert Dreyfuss. "In this case they're fighting for their lives."

Small business also wields big clout. With premiums 25 percent to 40 percent higher than those for larger firms, many don't provide coverage and don't want to be forced to. The wealthy pharmaceutical companies have so far been relatively quiet. But should a viable reform plan include coverage and cost controls on prescription drugs, "the drug companies will go crazy" and deploy their lobbyists to defeat it, warns Harvard's Blendon. That leaves the AMA at the forefront, where doctors will retain their traditional activist role. "You underestimate the AMA's influence at your peril. They have truly awesome power," says AMA member Dr. Quentin Young.

All of the misery, however, may force Congress to enact some type of reform soon. "The issue of the uninsured is not enough to move the process," says one congressional aide. "But as the problem becomes worse for the middle class, for working people and people who vote, people will begin to say that this is not acceptable."

MEDICAL CARE AND
SOCIAL JUSTICE

THE MEDICAL INDUSTRY
SUPPORTS REFORM

Raymond Scalettar, M.D.

Raymond Scalettar has an active internal medicine practice in Washington, D.C., and is a trustee of the American Medical Association (AMA).

Points to Consider:

1. What are the causes of rapid growth in health care costs? How is our society to blame?

2. What benefits are there from these increased expenditures?

3. How is the AMA working for health care reform? Give several examples.

Excerpted from testimony given by Raymond Scalettar before the House Subcommittee on Health and the Environment of the Committee on Energy and Commerce, October 31, 1991.

We see the pain and illness of this population and we have put forward a comprehensive proposal to address these needs.

As care-givers, physicians witness the grim reality facing the uninsured. We see this population not as statistics, but as the women, men and children who seek our help at emergency departments, clinics and offices. We see the pain and illness of this population and we have put forward a comprehensive proposal to address these needs.

Major Factors

Without question, a significant percentage of the growth in expenditures for medical and health care services reflects the circumstances in the United States where physicians and other health care professionals are able to provide our citizens with a breadth and quality of care that was not even imagined a few short years ago.

It also is important to note that American health care expenditures reflect spending for social services and medical care due to problems in our society including crimes, drugs and poverty. In addition, our health care system provides services and is held accountable for expenses that are incurred in providing care that ideally is avoidable. For example:

- According to a study published in the September 18, 1991, issue of *JAMA*, annual hospital costs for babies born in the, U.S. to cocaine-using mothers are approaching $500 million; and

- Based on an analysis of 1985 expenses for the cost of injury in the U.S., published by the Centers for Disease Control in 1989, approximately $5.3 billion was spent for direct medical expenses stemming from assault ($2.4 billion) and self-inflicted injuries ($2.9 billion).

Before turning to our recommendations regarding health care reform, it should be clearly understood that money spent for avoidable health care needs is just the tip of expenses arising from factors such as drug use and violence. Demonstrated by the sales volume of tobacco products and the continued violence we inflict on one another, such expenditures unfortunately are sure to continue.

NO LONGER ACCEPTABLE

The Journal of the American Medical Association (JAMA) *urged the federal government to guarantee basic medical insurance to all Americans, saying it is "no longer acceptable morally, ethically or economically" for the 31 million to 37 million citizens to live with inadequate or non-existent health insurance.*

Using uncharacteristically strong language, it also blamed "longstanding, systematic, institutionalized" racism, including that of organized medicine, for the fact that most of the uninsured and under-insured are members of minority groups. And it called the status quo "morally unacceptable".

News Service, "AMA Urges Guaranteed Basic Health Insurance", Minneapolis **Star-Tribune,** May 14, 1991

Cost-Effectiveness

Our health care system is costly. It continues to require more and more of our resources. The current tax structure and the health insurance system actually encourage the use of services. Furthermore, this occurs in a country where the citizens expect and routinely receive access to the most technically advanced health care in the world.

The cost of health care services is driven by many factors—including new and improved technology, aggregate population growth, more health-conscious consumers who utilize more services and technology, inflation, and the health problems associated with increasing societal problems such as AIDS, violence and drug abuse. The AMA maintains a number of key activities that address the "cost" dimension of health care through various measures that respond to many of these factors.

Practice Guidelines —The AMA supports measures that will enhance the value of every health care dollar spent. For example, the AMA is a leader in the development of practice guidelines, and is working with the nation's medical specialties and the Agency for Health Care Policy and Research on this important issue. Appropriately developed parameters, which will identify the medical consensus on the most effective treatment strategies for a given medical condition, will enhance the value of health care by helping to eliminate ineffective treatments and care.

Technology Assessment and Outcomes Research—We support outcomes research and technology assessment to determine the effectiveness of medical treatments. The AMA devotes significant resources to technology assessment through

its Diagnostic and Therapeutic Technology Assessment (DATTA) program. Since 1982, DATTA has been evaluating the safety and effectiveness of drugs, devices, procedures and techniques used in the practice of medicine. DATTA draws from a panel of 2,500 expert physicians who evaluate new and emerging technologies. The results of these assessments are communicated to practicing physicians and more than 1,150 health care organizations, primarily through AMA publications.

Essential Benefits in Lieu of State Mandates—The AMA endorses employer-required insurance instead of state-required or mandated health care coverage. In lieu of such mandates, which often require very expensive packages, employers should be required to provide a minimum, less costly, essential benefits package such as the one the AMA has developed.

Liability Reform—The AMA supports federal reform of the medical liability system. The estimated $20.7 billion, a conservative figure, attributable to defensive medicine and liability insurance premiums in 1989 is staggering. These costs contribute significantly to the access problem by causing physicians to abandon certain procedures and areas of the country. This access problem has reached its extreme in states such as Georgia, where 57 counties have no providers of obstetric care.

Antitrust Protection—The AMA supports allowing local medical societies to review and arbitrate patient complaints about fees and other matters. Under present Federal Trade Commission (FTC) interpretation, effective peer fee review is unlikely. Amendment of federal antitrust laws is needed to allow local medical societies to conduct reviews of excessive fees without the fear of antitrust liability.

Health Promotion—The AMA supports health promotion and preventive health measures such as the Cancer Screening Incentive Act of 1991. Society must be made aware of the severe and costly effects of inadequate shelter and lifestyle choices such as smoking, substance abuse, poor nutrition and lack of exercise. We cannot afford to overlook the value of general health education and the need for continued promotion of family values. The AMA strongly supports and lobbies for health effects advertising, effective hand gun control and restrictions on tobacco and alcohol promotion.

Administrative Expenditures—All insurers, including self-insurers, should utilize a uniform claim form such as the one developed by the Uniform Claim Form Task Force (chaired by the AMA) and used by the Medicare program. There also should be a standardized format for electronic claims.

Cost-sharing—Over-insurance needs to be discouraged. To aid consumers in meeting personal health care expenses, they should have the option of spending funds deposited in a flexible benefit account (an IRA for health care purposes). There also should be a limit on the favorable tax treatment of employer-provided coverage. An average of $12 billion per year over five years would go far to meet the needs of the uninsured.

Portability/Continuity—Once covered through employment, an employee (and dependents) who leaves that employment should have the guarantee of future coverage, with no waiting period or pre-existing condition limitation, with a new employer without any rate increase (other than due to geographic location) to the employer or employee due to health condition.

Community Rating/Open Enrollment—Premiums charged to small business should be comparable (no more than 10 percent higher) to the per capita average across all the group insurance sold in the same community for the same benefit package during the preceding three months. Open enrollment should be required.

Benefits/reinsurance — Every insurer should be required to offer one policy with the exact required basic benefits (no more, no less).

Full Support

The growth in expenditures for medical and health care services reflects the reality in the United States where physicians and other health care professionals and providers are able to provide our citizens with a breadth and quality of care that was not even imagined a few short years ago. Meeting this need has resulted in the U.S. clearly being recognized as the leader in the development of health care technologies and services, and for our citizens, being more productive in their daily activities.

In conclusion, we recognize that cost containment initiatives need to be nurtured now if we are to have reasonable expectations that health care reform actions of the future are to succeed. However, difficulty in reducing the growth of costs needs to be recognized. While the AMA fully supports efforts to root out spending for unnecessary services, efforts to accomplish this goal should not be made at the expense of patients.

10 MEDICAL CARE AND SOCIAL JUSTICE

GREED AND THE PHARMACEUTICAL INDUSTRY: Points and Counterpoints

Gerald J. Mossinghoff vs. David Pryor

Gerald J. Mossinghoff is President of the Pharmaceutical Manufacturers Association (PMA). The PMA represents more than 100 research-based pharmaceutical companies that discover, develop and produce most prescription drugs in the U.S. and many medicines used in other countries. David Pryor is a U.S. senator from the state of Arkansas and is chairman of the Special Senate Committee on Aging.

Points to Consider:

1. Why is research and development (R&D) so important?

2. How do medicines save money as well as lives?

3. How much money is spent on research? On marketing?

4. What was the average profit for the pharmaceutical industry?

5. Why does David Pryor feel the drug companies' research and development argument is weak? Explain.

Excerpted from the testimony of Gerald J. Mossinghoff and David Pryor before the Senate Committee on Labor and Human Resources, October 16, 1991.

THE POINT

Gerald J. Mossinghoff

The pharmaceutical industry is a premier high-technology industry — where today's business creates tomorrow's therapeutic breakthroughs. It is a highly innovative industry that has long led the world in discovering and developing new medicines.

It also is a highly competitive industry. The sales of the four largest Pharmaceutical Manufacturers Association (PMA) firms account for only 25 percent of total domestic sales. The top eight firms account for less than 50 percent of the U.S. market. And the sales of 20 companies must be combined to reach 75 percent of the market. The industry has consistently maintained a positive balance of trade — which was $1.4 billion in 1990 according to the Department of Commerce.

Research and Development

To remain innovative and competitive, the industry invests huge sums in research and development. R&D expenditures by PMA firms have doubled every five years since 1970. In 1991, the industry is expected to invest $9.2 billion in R&D — once again more than the National Institute of Health spends on all biomedical research.

This year, the industry is investing 16.9 percent of its sales in research and development — while all industries engaged in research and development on average invest less than four percent of sales in R&D, according to the National Science Foundation.

The enormous increase in R&D expenditures is in part attributable to the uncertainty of success and the increasing costs of discovering and developing a new drug. Only about one out of every 5,000 compounds that are synthesized and tested in the laboratory becomes a marketable product. And it takes an average of 10 to 12 years to discover and develop a new drug. The average cost of discovering and developing a new drug is now estimated to exceed $230 million, up sharply from previous estimates. This rising cost of developing a new drug reflects the fact that, among other factors, pharmaceutical companies are concentrating more on discovering drugs to treat complex chronic diseases, drugs that require longer development times.

Spending on Drugs

It is well known that spending on health care has been increasing rapidly as a percentage of Gross National Product (GNP), but it is less well known that spending on drugs as a percentage of GNP has remained relatively constant. Health care spending – just over seven percent of GNP in 1970 – reached 12.2 percent of GNP in 1990, according to the Health Care Financing Administration (HCFA), while spending on prescription drugs remained substantially under one percent of GNP – just as it has for the past 25 years.

Worldwide Leader

Our industry is the source of nearly all new drugs in the U.S. and the leading source worldwide. Of the 100 most prescribed patented drugs in the U.S., 94 were patented by private industry. Forty-seven of the 97 new drugs marketed worldwide between 1975 and 1989 originated in the U.S., more than three times the number from any other country.

Most Cost-Effective Therapy

Medicines not only save lives – they save money. Medicines are the most cost-effective form of medical therapy because they help to reduce the cost of alternative, more expensive forms of medical care, such as surgery and hospitalization.

A recent study by the Battelle Medical Technology and Policy Research Center found that the use of pharmaceuticals saved 1.6 million lives and $141 billion over the past 50 years for just four diseases – tuberculosis, polio, coronary heart disease and cerebrovascular disease. Battelle also projected that during the next 25 years, the use of pharmaceuticals will save $68 billion in

U.S. health care costs for Alzheimer's disease, while reducing the number of severe cases by almost 400,000. In addition, $211 billion will be saved in costs for cardiovascular disease with five million deaths and nine million cases avoided. Further, $180 billion in costs will be saved for arthritis, and the number of disabling rheumatoid arthritis cases will be reduced by half and the number of osteoarthritis cases by more than 20 percent.

New Medicines in Development

Despite the progress that has been made in curing disease and the prospects for future advances, many diseases remain untreated. The research-based pharmaceutical industry provides the best hope for finding new and better treatments. According to a recent PMA survey, research-based pharmaceutical companies are involved in developing 329 medicines for diseases that primarily afflict older Americans. The health care costs of these diseases are staggering.

Alzheimer's disease, arthritis, cancer, cardiovascular diseases, depression, diabetes and osteoporosis are estimated to cost $385 billion a year in the U.S. alone. This enormous figure fortunately will be reduced, as many of the 299 medicines in development to prevent, cure or treat these seven diseases are approved and marketed. Fifty-nine of those 299 drugs are now awaiting approval at the FDA.

COUNTERPOINT

Senator David Pryor

Any time Congress is critical of the enormous profit margins of the pharmaceutical industry, or questions the need for the industry to raise prices in excess of three times the rate of inflation, the industry argues that they need these exorbitant profits and high prices to finance research and development. However, it is clear that their well-worn and re-recycled research and development argument is not going to sell anymore. Consider these facts:

FACT 1: Americans are already providing hundreds of millions of dollars in tax breaks annually for the industry's R&D investment.

FACT 2: According to a 1991 *Forbes Magazine* article, the drug industry is spending a BILLION DOLLARS MORE a year on marketing than it is on research; that is, the industry will spend $10 billion on marketing and advertising this year, but only $9 billion on research and development.

KICKBACKS

Health care provides many opportunities for kickbacks for steering business to suppliers, pharmacies or laboratories. A medical equipment supplier might pay off a hospital to get a monopoly on its business, or slip cash to a doctor in return for patient referrals; a pharmacy may pay "incentives" for a nursing home to steer patients its way; labs may reward doctors for a stream of patient referrals.

Gordon Witkin, "Health Care Fraud", **U.S. News & World Report,** February 24, 1992

FACT 3: After accounting for the investment in research and development, the pharmaceutical industry still earns an annual *Fortune 500* industry-leading profit of 15.4 percent. This industry profit average is triple that of the average *Fortune 500* club member, which is 4.6 percent.

FACT 4: The drug industry says it needs such profits to attract capital. Yet they certainly do not need a return on shareholder investments (return on equity) that industry analysts say is consistently 50 percent higher than the average *Fortune 500* company to attract capital. Other *Fortune 500* companies, whose profit margins are one-third that of the drug industry, do not appear to have trouble attracting sufficient capital.

FACT 5: In addition to the hundreds of millions of dollars in direct research and development tax breaks given to the drug industry each year, a significant amount of research on new drug products occurs in federal facilities or with grants provided by federal agencies. For example, most of the research on the drug AZT, used to treat symptoms of AIDS, was conducted at the National Institute of Health (NIH), yet a private drug company holds the patent on the product and has used the patent to charge exorbitant prices for the drug.

FACT 6: The drug companies whose R&D investments have brought no new breakthrough drugs to market are the very same companies that are increasing prices at some of the highest rates. Therefore, while there are some drug companies which are research intensive, the majority are using the "research" argument as the excuse to raise prices, yet their research pipeline is dry. For example:

● Dilantin, manufactured by Parke-Davis, has been on the

market since 1953. Since 1985, it has gone up in price 69 percent, an annual average increase of over 11 percent. Parke-Davis has not brought one new molecular entity to market in the last five years.

FACT 7: For a pharmaceutical company that spends 15 percent of its revenue on research to increase its research expenditures by 10 percent, it would only require a 1.5 percent increase in its drug prices each year. However, drug manufacturers have been increasing prices, on average, at three times the rate of inflation for the last eleven years.

FACT 8: One of the largest investors in R&D in the industry—Merck—is holding its price increases to inflation. If the world's most research-intensive drug company can adopt this responsible public policy, the others should be able to do the same.

FACT 9: In Canada, the drug industry has voluntarily agreed to limit its price increases to the inflation rate, while substantially increasing its investment in research.

EXAMINING COUNTERPOINTS

This activity may be used as an individualized study guide for students in libraries and resource centers or as a discussion catalyst in small group and classroom discussions.

The Point:

Hospital "dumping" is repeated 250,000 times a year in the U.S. when hospitals turn away sick and injured people or women in labor due to a lack of medical insurance or other inability to pay their bill. There is no justification for emergency rooms to refuse treatment to the poor. Hospitals that wish to make money in a community have a responsibility to help care for all its sick and injured. And that community has a responsibility to help that hospital meet the expense of patients who cannot pay. The decision to treat a patient should be a medical decision based on moral and ethical principles, not an economic decision based on profit.

The Counterpoint:

Private hospitals are in business to make a profit. No one questions the right of any other private firm to make money. Yet, hospitals seeking financial reward are deemed unethical. The equipment and services provided for patients by the modern hospital cost money. You simply cannot offer free services and stay in business for long. Hospitals should no more be forced to provide free treatment for those who cannot pay their bill, than a restaurant should be forced to feed the unemployed. Hospitals already provide more than their share of charity. Forcing such policies will only lead to a reduction in emergency room services, forcing needy patients to seek treatment elsewhere.

Guidelines

Social issues are usually complex, but often problems become oversimplified in political debates and discussion. Usually a polarized version of social conflict does not adequately represent the diversity of views that surround social conflicts.

1. Examine the counterpoints above. Then write down possible interpretations of this issue other than the two arguments stated in the counterpoints above.

2. Who do you think ultimately pays for patients who cannot pay their bills?

3. How does the Hippocratic Oath fit into this debate?

4. How do the principles of a free market system relate?

5. Which readings in this book parallel these counterpoints? How?

6. What are your own opinions on this debate?

CHAPTER 3

HEALTH CARE OPTIONS: IDEAS IN CONFLICT

HEALTH CARE OPTIONS: IDEAS IN CONFLICT

HEALTH CARE REFORM: AN OVERVIEW

In 1992 over 30 million Americans were without health insurance coverage. Lack of health benefits coverage may result in individuals not seeking or not being able to obtain health care services; exposure to medical care expenses that may consume an individual or family's income and savings; shifting of costs from those who cannot pay to others who can; or services being provided in inappropriate settings, such as non-emergency health care in emergency rooms.

Numerous bills have been introduced in the 102nd Congress to expand health insurance coverage. The generic approaches embodied in these bills include instituting a **universal health** insurance system; **mandating employers** to extend health insurance benefits to uncovered or underinsured groups; **expanding health insurance coverage** through Medicaid or Medicare; and providing tax incentives to provide coverage privately.

Universal access proposals have generally taken one of three approaches: a social insurance program modelled after that of Canada or Western European nations in which services are primarily financed through general revenues but are furnished by independent providers; a national health service like the British National Health Service in which the government both finances and furnishes health care services; and a mixed public-private program in which the government shares the financing burden with employers, but health services would continue to be furnished by independent providers.

Excerpted from a CRS Report for Congress titled, "Health Insurance Legislation", July 1, 1991.

Employment-based options could be used to provide coverage to more persons or to improve coverage already provided by employers. Federal initiatives could take the form of a federal mandate on employers to provide coverage or pay a portion of public plan coverage for their workers, or federal requirements on existing health insurance plans to reach greater numbers of people, or to provide specific benefits.

Existing public programs, such as Medicare and Medicaid, could be expanded to reach a larger population. For example, some proposals would extend Medicare to the entire population, providing a universal social insurance program. Federal or state tax might be modified in a variety of ways to help more individuals purchase health insurance or to encourage more employers to provide group health plans. In addition, bills have been introduced that are designed to make private health insurance more affordable or available through reform of the private health insurance market.

NATIONAL HEALTH CARE IS THE ANSWER

Edie Rasell

Edie Rasell wrote this article on universal health care for Z Papers, *a quarterly publication of* Z Magazine.

Points to Consider:

1. What would be the major components of a universal health care plan? Who would be covered?

2. How would such a national plan be financed?

3. Why has the market method failed at cost containment?

4. What is the RBRVS and how would it work?

Edie Rasell, "Health Care", **Z Papers,** January/March, 1992.

An equitable and affordable health insurance system would have a single payer. There would be one source of health insurance and all necessary services would be covered.

The U.S. health care system is in crisis. High administrative expenses, primarily the costs imposed by the over 1,200 private health insurance carriers, absorb up to 24 percent of the total health care dollar. For each person who comes in contact with the health care system, detailed bills must be submitted; claims must be checked and approved; someone must verify that deductibles have been met, co-payments made, prior authorizations obtained, etc. The health care system is being buried in paperwork.

Our health costs are very high, and the distribution of these costs among people in different income classes also needs radical revision. Heavy financial burdens are imposed on those least able to afford them. Because it is so expensive, access to health care in the U.S. depends in large part upon having insurance coverage, either private insurance, Medicare or Medicaid. But even among those who do have health insurance, many people feel very insecure about their ongoing access to care.

Unemployment often brings the complete loss of health insurance. Changing employers can mean that pre-existing health conditions are no longer insured under a new policy. A major illness in a worker employed in a small company can cause premiums for all employees in the firm to rise to unaffordable levels. Some entire industries have been blacklisted by private insurance companies and the workers declared uninsurable.

System in Crisis

The U.S. health care system, while in some ways the best in the world, is in a crisis which will not be eased by tinkering at the margins. Only major, comprehensive reform will solve the problems of restricted access and high cost. Such a reform would be based on four principles:

*Universal Access   *Cost Containment

*A Single Payer   *Equitable Financing

Health Insurance for All

In an equitable health insurance system, all necessary health care services (including preventive and acute care, diagnostic and therapeutic procedures, long term and mental health care, substance abuse treatment, dental and vision services, prescription drugs and necessary medical appliances) would be available to everyone as an entitlement—not because employers choose to sponsor health insurance for workers and their families—but because a humane society ensures that all people have access to health care.

The provision of health insurance must be separated from the employer/employee relationship. Access to health care must not be jeopardized when people change jobs, leave the labor force, become part time or temporary workers, or are unemployed.

It is important that all necessary services be insured, because otherwise the new system will permit the recurrence of a problem common today. People needing services not covered by the insurance plan eventually receive them (because we are a humane society), but providers are not reimbursed. This puts budgetary pressures on the hospitals or doctors who perform this "charity" care. If reimbursement is not available, then those who provide these services will be placed in financial jeopardy, as are many of our urban hospitals today.

Non-citizens must also be covered. Visitors will be asked to pay for services received (as they are now). For visitors from a country that has a social insurance plan or a national health service (and there are many), the reimbursement would come through reciprocal arrangements made between the U.S. system and plans in other countries. If people are unable to pay in full and there is no health insurance system in their country to pay the costs, then insurance funds specifically designated for this purpose should be used to reimburse providers.

Providing coverage to those who are currently uninsured or underinsured will not raise total health costs excessively, especially compared to the $67 billion to be saved by cutting administrative waste. Expanding service to the uninsured at an estimated cost of $12 billion and to the underinsured for a additional $37 billion, would still leave $18 billion for transition costs and new programs.

A Single Pay System

An equitable and affordable health insurance system would have a single payer. There would be one source of health

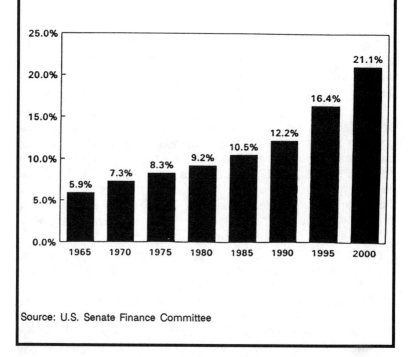

Health Expenditure as a Percent of GNP
1965-2000

Source: U.S. Senate Finance Committee

insurance (similar to Medicare for the over-65 today) and all
necessary services would be covered. All health care bills would
be paid by a single payer, thus greatly simplifying the claims
procedure and reducing the paper shuffling necessary to
determine responsibility for payment. The single payer is the sole
purchaser of health care services, and therefore has some ability
to set prices. The advantages of this system are its administrative
simplicity and efficiency, and its ability to exert some control
over prices charged by providers.

In a single payer system, private insurance firms are
prohibited from writing policies for any services covered by the
social insurance plan. This is to prevent the wealthy from "opting
out" of the public system, leading to a loss of political support

and reductions in funding which weaken the system as has happened in the U.K. Opponents of the single payer system say it is politically impossible; it is not culturally acceptable in the U.S. to have a large public program. However, polls show that a majority of people favor a single payer system over the current U.S. arrangements.

Another argument against this system is "we can't afford it." This is a smoke screen. The system is cheaper and would save substantial amounts of money starting immediately in the first year. In the aggregate we would spend less on health care under this payment and financing structure. However, it would require more money to be channelled through the tax system. This is a problem for conservatives who wish to reduce the role of government.

Cost Containment Measures

Only in the U.S. are physician and hospital fees determined, by and large, in "the market", although in recent years insurers, particularly Medicare, are placing more restrictions on charges. Purists would have us believe that markets always provide the best possible economic outcomes. In this view, competition among suppliers to sell their goods and maximize their profits ensure that we pay the lowest possible prices for the highest quality goods. But there is no market for medical services in the traditional sense. Demand is determined not by consumers but by physicians in their recommendations to patients. And physicians are also the suppliers of the services.

There are potential conflicts of interest here. People do not shop around for the cheapest surgeon, physician, or medicine. Even if they did, they are ill-equipped to judge the quality of the medical care delivered. By and large we are willing to pay any price and obtain any test if we think our health is at stake. And many people pay only a small portion of their health care bills, so cost is a small consideration. In this context, arguing that we can rely on the market to restrain prices is not credible.

In an equitable and affordable single payer system, the government as sole purchaser of medical care uses its bargaining power with providers to hold down cost increases. We can learn from other countries some of the ways this can be done. Although other industrialized nations vary in the way their health care system is structured, in each country health care expenditures constitute a much smaller share of GNP than in the U.S., and all the countries use similar methods to contain costs.

A major instrument of cost containment is annually-negotiated national budgets for hospitals and for doctors' payments. Annual budgets — essentially expenditure caps — are determined for each hospital based on projected utilization of services. These budgets encourage hospitals to become more efficient.

An annual global budget for all doctors' services is also established. The budget places a cap on annual physician reimbursement and ensures that targets are not exceeded. Once total expenditures are determined and projected utilization estimated, fees for services can be calculated. Just as today, most doctors and hospitals would remain in the private sector and doctors would continue to be reimbursed on a fee-for-service basis.

We should use the newly developed Resource Based Relative Value Scale (RBRVS) to determine relative fees for doctors' services and procedures. The RBRVS is the result of an extensive process to determine the relative knowledge, training, and skill requirements for every procedure and physician service. This work has found that surgical procedures are reimbursed at too high a rate relative to "thinking" skills such as consultations by internal medicine specialists. Paying physicians in accordance with the RBRVS will increase compensation for preventive and diagnostic services and reduce compensation for surgical procedures.

Cost Sharing

A common cost containment measure practiced in the U.S. and to a lesser extent in some European countries is to require users of health care to pay a fee at the point of service. The goal of any such fees should be to promote efficiency within the health care delivery system and to decrease unnecessary utilization. It is not clear that cost sharing would have any effect on either of these.

Cost sharing has its biggest impact on the poor, who are the first to decrease their utilization out of cost considerations. But these people are more likely to fall ill than are members of the middle class, and it would be bad policy to create more barriers inhibiting their access to care. Cost sharing should be eliminated. It raises administrative costs, is a barrier to access for the poor and potentially the middle class, and is at best only marginally effective at containing costs.

Pay Through Taxes

Although for accounting purposes there are generally considered to be four "payers" of health care costs—federal and state governments, business and individuals, (insurers just function as intermediaries), the costs ultimately are all paid by workers and taxpayers.

An equitable and affordable health insurance system should receive its revenue from progressive income taxes. Funding through payroll taxes would be less desirable, but minimally should include a wage floor to ease the burden for the poor, and no wage ceiling.

Conclusion

Americans are not healthy. Not because we lack the technological and financial means to be healthy, but because important aspects of our culture and institutions are inimical to well-being, the delivery system is seriously flawed, and access to care and financing is inequitable and irrational. A growing percentage of the population lacks access to care and are burdened by excessive costs. I have focused on a solution to the most glaring problem which could be implemented immediately. The health care system described here, based on universal access, a single payer, cost containment measures, and progressive financing would be a major step toward providing equitable and affordable care for all.

A FREE MARKET SYSTEM IS
THE ANSWER

Terree P. Wasley

Terree Wasley is a Washington-based economist and free-lance writer who has worked on tax and health care issues for the U.S. Chamber of Commerce, the Goldwater Institute and the Heritage Foundation.

Points to Consider:

1. How does the author describe government intervention in our health care system?

2. What has been the fate of socialized medicine in other nations? Give several examples.

3. Why must we maintain a free-market approach?

Terree P. Wasley, "The Coming Push for National Health Care", **The Freeman**, January 1990.

Now is the time to reverse the trend toward nationalizing our health care system and replace it with a free market.

Now is the time to propose major reforms to this country's ailing health care system, bringing it back into balance with our free-market convictions. The time may be right to urge significant changes that would curtail spiraling health care costs, making health care more affordable and offering citizens the chance to choose the way to provide for their own future health care needs.

The administration must act now, for to wait may allow an opportunity to pass that might never come again. Those who believe government can best provide for our lives are already working behind the scenes for passage of a comprehensive national health care plan for all Americans.

Calls for some kind of national health care program have increased during the past years and are coming from a variety of sources. The rapid escalation in health care costs, particularly in the 1980s, and attention to the fact that approximately 30 million Americans lack health care insurance, have raised demands for some kind of universal solution.

Strange Bedfellows

What has amazed some are voices from the business community speaking out for more federal government involvement in health care. Ever-rising health care costs, due to government interference and a perverse system of incentives and controls, have so frustrated American business leaders that some have now resigned themselves to failure and are asking the government to bail them out.

Art Puccini, vice president at General Electric said, "rising employee medical costs may lead some of us who today are free-market advocates to re-examine our thinking and positions with respect to government-sponsored national health insurance." Ford Motor Company has been using its seat on President Bush's competitiveness council to push for government health care, and General Motors vice president Beach Hall has been seen at several recent Capital Hill meetings on the issue.

Walter B. Maher, director of employee benefits for Chrysler Corporation, has urged that a national budget be set for health care each year — much like in Canada, Britain, and other countries with national health care plans. The Washington

Reprinted by permission: **Tribune Media Services**

Business Group on Health, which represents about 180 Fortune 500 companies on health issues, is one of several groups drafting a national health care plan with the goal of controlling health-related spending.

Astonishingly, it's not just big business, frustrated with mounting health care costs, that is turning a favorable eye toward a national health plan. A recent Dun & Bradstreet survey of small business found that 38 percent favored some form of national health insurance. The Independent Business Federation says 15 percent of its members polled in 1989 would agree to a mandatory national health insurance program.

In addition to business, another unlikely group has joined the clamor for national health care: physicians. In 1989, Physicians for a National Health Program, a two-year-old group of 1,200 doctors from across the U.S., proposed a single public insurance plan that would pay for all approved medical services. According to Dr. Arnold Relman, editor-in-chief of the *New England Journal of Medicine,* "Nothing short of a comprehensive plan is likely to achieve the goals of universal access, cost containment and preservation of quality that everyone seems to want."

Socialized Medicine

Many experts believe that it is currently impossible to undertake a national health care program of any kind, because of federal budget deficits. Despite this, polls are showing that Americans see the deficit as less and less of a threat and that they are concerned about those who don't have access to health care because of its current high costs. Because of that concern, and if skyrocketing health costs are not slowed, some health care experts, such as Harvard University professor Robert J. Blendon, predict that national health care will [continue to be] a major issue.

Socialized medicine, the term normally used for a national care program, conjures up vivid images in most American minds. One sees Soviet citizens dying because of a lack of adequate medical care, British citizens waiting for months to undergo a simple procedure or surgery, rich Europeans paying under the table to get their names pushed to the top of a waiting list, and Canadians hopping the border into the U.S. to have procedures done, rather than wait months or maybe years in their homeland.

No one, including most members of Congress, expects the American people to accept a socialized system like that of the former Soviet Union, with its centralized control of every aspect of health care. Recent attention given to the severe problems besieging the British national health care system prompted Prime Minister Thatcher to institute some market-based reforms. However, many bills recently introduced in Congress would provide for a system of national health insurance modeled after the perceived success of the Canadian health care system.

The Canada Comparison

Many politicians have praised the Canadian system of health care as successful in providing satisfactory health care at lower costs than in the United States. But the problems inherent in any health system based on social insurance or direct government funding are already showing up in the Canadian program. These endemic flaws should give pause to U.S. lawmakers eager to adopt a plan similar to the Canadian one.

The underlying problem with any social insurance system is that patients make little or no contribution to the cost of their care. What follows is the exorbitant increase in the demand for health care services, and the resulting price controls, rationing, income controls on physicians, shortages of equipment, deterioration of medical facilities, and long waiting lists. Canada has exhibited all of these symptoms, and many Canadians routinely cross the border into the U.S. for treatment. Price controls, rationing, and waiting lists do put a lid on health care spending, and that is exactly why many politicians can boast that Canada spends less on health care than the United States. But is that the quality of health care Americans want?

Now is the time to reverse the trend toward nationalizing our health care system and replace it with a free market. The creation of Medicare and Medicaid in the 1960s, their continued expansion, and the addition of a crazy quilt of health care programs by both the federal and state governments have virtually destroyed American access to reasonable and efficient health care.

Free Market

Government intervention has our health care system caught in a vicious cycle of government-encouraged demand that drives up costs, bankrupts federal and state budgets, and leads to still more infusions of money and program expansions that encourage additional consumption. Only the elimination of government interference and a return to a free market in health care will end the move toward nationalization. Only a free market will break the spiral of ever-increasing medical costs. As Ludwig von Mises wrote, "The pricing process of the unhampered market directs production into those channels in which it best serves the wishes of the consumers as manifested on the market." Only a free market in health care will allow individuals maximum choice in meeting their health care needs.

HEALTH CARE OPTIONS:
IDEAS IN CONFLICT

EMPLOYERS MUST BEAR RESPONSIBILITY FOR HEALTH COVERAGE

Karen Davis

Karen Davis is professor and chair of the Department of Health Policy and Management at Johns Hopkins School of Hygiene and Public Health, Baltimore, Maryland.

Points to Consider:

1. What is the basic concept of a "play-or-pay" health plan?

2. What options would be available to employers? Describe them.

3. How would children and women benefit? The poor?

4. How would costs be affected? Employment?

Excerpted from testimony by Karen Davis before the U.S. Senate Committee on Labor and Human Resources, July 24, 1991.

Health-America gives employers the choice of enrolling workers and their families in either private health plans or in a public plan.

The nation can no longer tolerate the hardship imposed by a health system that leaves 33 million Americans uninsured, 60 million with inadequate health insurance, and virtually all Americans at risk of being unable to afford decent health care if they lose their jobs or become seriously ill.

The ["play-or-pay" concept] has much to commend it. It would build on our existing system of employer-provided health insurance — closing the gaps in coverage by requiring all employers to provide either *private health insurance* or pay a payroll tax toward coverage of workers and dependents under a *new public health plan*. It distributes the financial burden of care more equitably among employers and among individuals by giving everyone the option of coverage under a plan where contributions are based on income. It makes health care affordable to everyone — including low-wage firms and individuals with modest incomes or serious chronic health conditions.

Health-America

The Health-America plan builds on the American tradition of a combination of employer-provided health insurance coverage for workers and their families and public plan coverage for those requiring special assistance. Building on this structure, it proposes a fundamental strengthening and integration of our mixed private-public system of health insurance coverage to guarantee coverage to all Americans. There are many innovative features of this plan which I think deserve special attention.

Employer Choice

One of the most innovative features of Health-America is that it gives employers the choice of enrolling workers and their families in either private health plans or in a public plan. Those employers who currently have private health insurance coverage that adequately meets the needs of their workers and families would be unaffected. However, those employers who find it difficult to obtain good private health insurance at a reasonable cost would have the option of simply paying a payroll tax to ensure coverage of workers and dependents under a public program.

This employer choice approach has several advantages. It

"The operation was a success—but your life savings only have 30 days to live."

makes coverage more affordable for low-wage firms – by limiting the maximum liability to a percentage of payroll such as seven percent. This contribution would be known with certainty, would be predictable over time, and would be more affordable for a low-wage firm than a premium contribution covering the full cost of coverage. It eliminates the time and administrative burden for a small firm to find a private health insurance plan, and gives firms the option of enrolling in a public plan whose administrative expenses typically run only two to three percent of benefit costs – contrasted with the 20-50 percent administrative costs built into many small firm health insurance premiums.

Public Plan Coverage Option

The public plan coverage option would also be extremely important to those outside the workforce or not strongly tied to the work force. Employers could cover part-time, temporary, and seasonal workers who are in and out of the workplace under the public plan. Unemployed workers could continue their coverage by picking up the premiums based on their ability to pay.

Most importantly, retired individuals or other non-working adults under age 65 would have the opportunity of buying in to a public plan before age 65. It would also improve coverage for those disabled individuals who now must wait at least two years for Medicare coverage. Spouses or widows of Medicare beneficiaries who are under 65 do not qualify for Medicare. Such individuals could purchase coverage with subsidies for the poor. This is an extremely important feature and should be considered for early implementation. Alternatively, Medicare coverage could be expanded to early retirees age 60 and over and the waiting period for the disabled could be shortened or eliminated.

Insurance Market Reform

Another attractive feature of Health-America is the proposed reform of the private health insurance market. This market is becoming increasingly selective—with insurers declining to cover individuals viewed to be poor health risks or instituting restrictions or waiting periods for pre-existing conditions. Small businesses, in particular, risk having their coverage dropped if a worker or family member becomes ill.

Under Health-America, private insurance plans could not exclude individuals or pre-existing conditions. It would require that the same coverage be offered to all firms on the same terms.

Medicaid and Children

The plan would replace the current Medicaid (health welfare) program with MediCare, a universal low-income entitlement program that is not tied to the welfare system. All poor persons would receive coverage without charge under this new federal public plan. Near-poor persons would be covered on a sliding scale basis.

The plan would begin by insuring all our nation's children. This places top priority on investing in the health of future generations by immediately assuring universal coverage of pregnant women and young children, with complete coverage of prenatal, well-baby care.

Costs

Total new health system cost is estimated at $18 billion when fully implemented. These outlays are modest given the current size of the health care sector. The proposed bill would add about three percent to total outlays for health care and make only marginal changes in current sources of financing. These are not revolutionary shifts in health outlays and could be expected to have only modest effects.

Impact on Employment

The employment effects of Health-America can be expected to be quite modest. The option of buying public plan coverage by paying a payroll tax such as seven percent of earnings guarantees employers that increases in labor costs cannot exceed this modest amount. Coverage is phased in, permitting small employers time to make corresponding adjustments in wages and other fringe benefits. In theory one would expect employers to shift costs in the longer term to workers, resulting in lower wages than would otherwise have been paid. The exception to this is those workers at or near the minimum wage where the employer could not legally lower wages.

Most importantly, the additional health services-received by the uninsured under this plan would in themselves have an employment-stimulating effect. The increased utilization or health services by the uninsured could be expected to add jobs in the health sector. The net employment impact of the bill, therefore, may be positive rather than negative. This should not be surprising since most new "spending" programs are expansionary rather than contractionary even when financed by additional revenues.

Implications for Health Care

This plan would add 33 million more people to health insurance coverage. This would provide much needed improvement in access to health care for a largely low-income population. Maternity and infant care services would be covered without cost-sharing by those covered. Improved access to acute care for the uninsured would improve health and give children a better chance at productive lives. The plan would help reduce the intolerable delay in obtaining needed health care for pregnant women, children, those with chronic health problems such as hypertension and diabetes, and those with life-threatening symptoms such as bleeding, chest pain, and loss of consciousness which many uninsured now experience.

While the cost and economic impact would be small relative to our nation's economic resources, the improved access to health care services would have a major impact on solving one of our nation's most pressing social problems. We are the only major industrialized nation that denies needed health care to its citizens because they are unable to afford such care. We cannot afford to waste the health and productive capacity of our people by failing to invest in adequate health care for all.

15   HEALTH CARE OPTIONS: IDEAS IN CONFLICT

CONSUMERS SHOULD BE RESPONSIBLE FOR HEALTH COVERAGE

Stuart M. Butler

Stuart M. Butler is Director of Domestic Policy Studies at The Heritage Foundation, a research organization in Washington, D.C. He has authored several books on welfare and urban issues including, "A National Health System for America".

Points to Consider:

1. Why are taxes a big part of our health care crisis?

2. Why are employer mandates like "play-or-pay" a bad idea?

3. What is the consumer approach?

4. How would this method of health care reform be financed?

Stuart M. Butler, "Time for a National Health System?", Public Policy Education Fund, Inc., Special Report No. 58, 1990.

The key is to use competition and consumer choice to "control" costs and influence providers.

Americans expect many things from their health care system. They demand state-of-the-art medicine, of course. But they also expect affordable access to adequate health care for everyone, regardless of income. They tend to feel that most government help to pay for care should go to those who need it most. And most believe that ultimate medical decisions should be made by the patient and his physician, not by some faraway bureaucrat.

With the exception of the quality of care for most Americans, which is the best in the world, the U.S. system falls short in every one of these areas. It is these deficiencies that have triggered the calls for basic reform. Unfortunately, most of the reforms now being touted in Washington, such as importing the Canadian system, would only make things worse.

Tax Problem

At the heart of the problem with the U.S. health system is the tax treatment of health costs. After World War II, the IRS ruled that the value of company-paid group health plans did not have to be included in a worker's taxable income.

This ruling was seen as a way of encouraging Americans to obtain health insurance, and it did trigger a rapid expansion of health insurance, ending the fear of crippling medical bills for millions of American families. But the tax policy has had two very undesirable side-effects.

The first is that with company plans picking up most or all of the tab, and with the premiums set for all of a firm's workers rather than for each individual, a physician has no incentive to consider cost when recommending a test or treatment to his patient, nor does the patient.

This lack of any incentive to economize means that price is not a barrier to good medicine, but it also has helped cause an explosion in health costs. The rate of price increases for medical care is about double the average inflation rate. This rapid rise in costs has led most employers to cut back on health plans, raising deductibles and, in some cases, dropping coverage for dependents—leading, in recent years, to bitter strikes over health benefits.

The second problem with the tax treatment of health care is that while company-provided coverage is tax-free without limit, there are virtually no tax benefits for health insurance or health

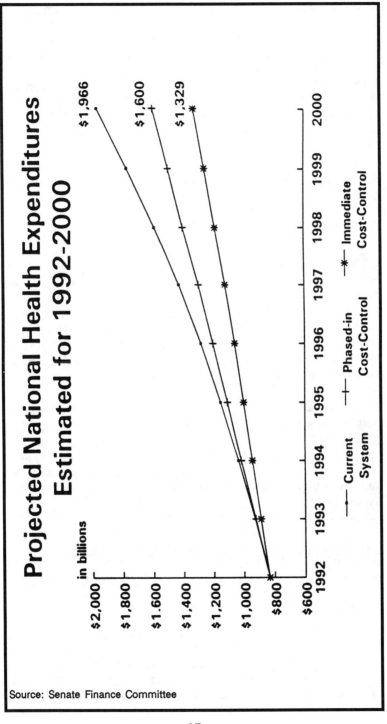

Projected National Health Expenditures Estimated for 1992-2000

in billions

$2,000
$1,800
$1,600
$1,400
$1,200
$1,000
$800
$600

1992 1993 1994 1995 1996 1997 1998 1999 2000

$1,966
$1,600
$1,329

—•— Current System

—+— Phased-in Cost-Control

—*— Immediate Cost-Control

Source: Senate Finance Committee

services purchased directly by a family. So if an employee in a small firm without a plan wishes to buy insurance, or a worker in a larger company wants to buy coverage for family members dropped from the company plan, he must pay in after-tax dollars. This means that the Chief Executive Officer (C.E.O.) of a Fortune 500 firm can obtain unlimited relief for a health plan that might include everything from dental flossing to marriage counseling, yet a minimum-wage worker in a small firm without a plan is given no tax relief if he buys a minimal insurance policy for his family.

This inequitable tax relief is the major reason that an estimated 37 million Americans lack any health insurance coverage at all, with millions more inadequately insured.

Don't Force Employers

Given the shortcomings of the U.S. health care system, the reforms proposed by liberal lawmakers look very attractive to many Americans. One popular idea would require all employers either to provide a standard health package for employees and their families or to pay a tax so that an equivalent package for their employees could be financed by government. In addition, companies would have to contribute to a fund to insure all Americans not otherwise covered by a company plan or by Medicaid or Medicare. Various versions of this system are referred to as "mandated benefits".

Appealing as these universal plans might seem, they suffer from serious drawbacks. Not only would they fail to provide a genuine solution to the deficiencies of the current U.S. system, but they would also undermine the high quality of that system. This is true because both the Canadian system and the mandated benefits approach seek to provide universal coverage by legislating access to care (through the public sector in Canada and the private sector under mandated benefits). And then, in an effort to contain the heavy demand for "free" care, government or private bureaucracies are used to control provider prices and patient access. Thus what is advertised as free access to the best possible care turns out to be rationing.

The Consumer Approach

The implicit assumption behind the liberal proposals is that markets really cannot function in the field of health care, and so decisions regarding the distribution of services must be put into the hands of government or corporate officials. In the liberal view of health care, consumer choice becomes an irritant, because it can circumvent the decisions of health planners.

Yet consumer choice in a competitive market is essential if resources are to be distributed efficiently and responsively to the desires of consumers. Central planning did not work in Eastern Europe and it does not work in health care. Moreover, consumer-driven markets can work very effectively in health care. To be sure, a man with a heart attack is not going to compare surgeon price lists while being rushed to a hospital in an ambulance. But that same man could make a very careful and informed choice about a health policy to deal with such an emergency, just as he might pick a life insurance policy.

By recognizing that markets can work in health care, it is possible to design a U.S. health care system that would remove the deficiencies of the existing system, and assure affordable access for all Americans, without the problems associated with liberal proposals. The key is to use competition and consumer choice to "control" costs and influence providers, just as markets do for other goods and services, and to focus government assistance on those who really need it to afford care.

Tax Reform

Such a market approach was developed by The Heritage Foundation and contains two basic elements. The first is a fundamental reform of the tax treatment of health care. Under the Heritage plan, the tax-free status of company-paid health plans would be phased out. The value of a health benefit provided by an employer would be added to the employee's taxable income, although this company would continue to deduct it as a labor cost. A new system of tax credits would be introduced into the personal tax code, so that each family would receive tax relief for buying health services or insurance.

The second element of the plan might be called a "social contract for health care". Under this contract, every American family would be required by law to obtain basic health insurance, including protection against catastrophic health costs, major medical care, and coverage for all family members. As its part of the contract, the government would agree to subsidize the purchase to the extent necessary, or to grant the family access to a public program. While such a mandate may seem an unwarranted intrusion, the fact is that society will not refuse medical care to those who need it. The mandate merely prevents individuals from becoming "free riders" by taking advantage of their neighbors.

This relatively simple reform would have a profound effect on the U.S. health care system, enabling the goal of universal access to medical care to be achieved without constructing a flawed national health service like that of Canada or Britain. Among the main effects:

1. The health cost spiral would be broken because consumers would have the incentive to choose the basic plan that delivers service with the best combination of quality and cost.

2. The tax credits would focus government help on those who really need it. The Fortune 500 top executive would receive little or no credit for health expenses and the office cleaner a large refundable credit.

3. The ultimate control over medical services would be with the patient. Each family would make basic decisions over such things as a choice of hospital and surgeon, and weigh these choices against the extra cost.

4. Some Americans actually favor employer-provided care or a national system precisely because there is little or no choice. They find health care so complex that they would rather have a knowledgeable person make choices for them. But under the

system of individual credits a family has every right to delegate choice to someone else.

The important point is that the family could join a plan offered by a group they trusted more than their employer. Perhaps a union plan; perhaps a plan from the farm bureau, a church, or an immigrants' organization; perhaps one tailored for individuals with specific needs, such as diabetics.

5. The very poor would be included in one of a number of ways. The refundable credits could reach to nearly 100 percent of reasonable health costs for the very poor, and so would in practice be a health voucher, replacing Medicaid.

This market-based strategy is explicitly designed to achieve the goals of a national health system: affordable access to health care for all citizens. In that narrow sense it may appear to be a concession to the liberal health agenda. But in reality it is a recognition that Americans believe that the country is rich enough and advanced enough to be able to guarantee its citizens adequate health care, through their own efforts or with society's help.

16 CASE STUDY: STATE HEALTH CARE PROGRAMS

STATES TAKE LEAD ON REFORM: An Overview

Susan Parker

Susan Parker, formerly the senior editor of New Physician magazine, *now works as a free-lance writer in Washington, D.C.*

Points to Consider:

1. Why are several states developing their own health care initiatives?

2. How successful have they been?

3. What is a key issue in Connecticut?

4. What approaches are being used by Massachusetts? By Connecticut, Hawaii, Oregon, Ohio?

Susan Parker, "The Basics of Health Care", **Sojourners,** November, 1990. Reprinted with permission from **Sojourners,** P.O. Box 29272, Washington, DC 20017.

The successes and failures of state initiatives may provide a roadmap for any far-reaching changes of the health care system in the United States.

The most significant work on reform in health coverage is taking place at the state level, according to several health policy experts. "States are fairly cynical about some kind of national health insurance program being enacted," says Dick Merritt, director of the Intergovernmental Health Policy Project in Washington, D.C., which monitors state health legislation. "As a result, they are taking the initiative."

Some of these plans could well serve as models for a national health insurance plan, according to Merritt and other experts in the health field. Unemployment and worker's compensation, for example, began at the state level, says Jack Needleman, a vice president at Lewin/ICF, a health care consulting firm. And the Canadian health care system, which some have touted as a model for the United States, was developed in the provinces.

State Initiatives

Several states are pursuing their own plans to expand coverage to people without health insurance. Many are experimenting with pilot projects such as setting up "risk pools", or funds where people without insurance can purchase coverage at a reasonable price. Some are expanding coverage through Medicaid, the state-federal program that provides health insurance to the disabled, poor women and children, and the poor elderly.

States such as Ohio and Washington are considering a "single payer" universal plan based on the Canadian model, which provides all of its citizens with a uniform set of health care services. A single government insurer has replaced private insurers to administer the plan, cutting down on overhead costs, supporters say.

Others, such as Hawaii and Massachusetts, have already enacted far-reaching changes to try to ensure universal coverage for all their citizens. And in perhaps the most controversial plan, Oregon officials are attempting to implement a plan that, among other things, could explicitly ration health care to the poor in return for a basic package of benefits.

States are anxious, for several reasons, to come to grips with the problem of providing health insurance. In the early 1980s, federal legislators spearheaded several laws that mandated

States get into health care act

States are moving ahead with their own health care plans, some similar to ones being considered at the federal level. How differing federal-state plans might mesh together remains unclear. States considering reform, and the type of plan:

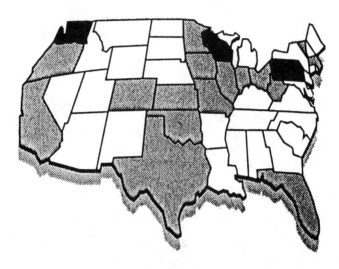

■ **Broader changes within existing systems:**
For example, plans such as "pay or play" with a combination of public/private coverage.

▨ **Public-run, single-payer, health care plans:**
Where federal or state government provides health coverage for all.

expansion of the Medicaid program to reach poor women and children in particular. Under Medicaid, states and the federal government share the costs of the program. Although the mandates provided greater coverage to some people, they also cost the states a great deal of money.

Realizing Limitations

States are also realizing the limitations of Medicaid. It covers only 40 percent of people in poverty, down from 63 percent in the mid-1970s. Prompted by the Reagan Administration, Congress imposed cuts in 1981 that resulted in the elimination of two million people from the Medicaid program. The federal government has also cut back its share of program payments, and states have tightened eligibility requirements, further reducing the number of people who receive Medicaid services.

Looking to the workplace to provide health insurance seems logical since about two-thirds of those without health insurance are working or are dependents of workers. That is the cornerstone of the Massachusetts plan, which is being closely watched by other states and by federal officials.

Massachusetts, like many other states that have taken health insurance initiatives, is attempting to build upon the existing public-private system, rather than overhaul the entire system as some have suggested. The Massachusetts plan requires most businesses to offer health insurance to their employees or contribute annually $1,680 per worker to a state insurance fund. In addition, businesses must pay $16.80 per employee into a fund that provides health insurance to people who are jobless.

Coverage for Everyone

Hawaii was the first state to enact legislation aimed at providing health care coverage for all its citizens. Since 1974, Hawaii has required that all employers offer insurance to those who work 20 or more hours a week. Employers also must pay at least half of the premium.

At least 22 states have set up task forces. These commissions typically include representatives of the insurance industry, the business community, the hospital association, and politicians—all of whom have interest groups they must defend, Needleman says. That often leaves little room for negotiation.

The Connecticut task force's recommendations did lead to a state law that includes subsidized insurance for pregnant women, children, and the disabled, as well as reforms in the insurance industry. Under one change, insurers will be prohibited from refusing to sell policies to small businesses or from raising premiums above a certain amount.

Rationing

Across the country in Oregon, meanwhile, state officials are trying to implement a controversial law that would explicitly ration health care to the poorest citizens in return for guaranteeing a basic level of services (See Chapter 4). The law is designed to ensure that everyone in the state, including 400,000 without insurance, has access to a basic package of health care services. It expands Medicaid coverage, requires employers to provide health care insurance, and establishes an insurance fund for people who are unable to obtain insurance.

The future of the Oregon plan is by no means certain. Before it can go into effect, the state must receive permission from the federal Health Care Financing Administration, which oversees Medicaid. Representative Waxman, one of the most powerful members of Congress, has criticized the plan and may try to block its implementation.

A Roadmap

Few states are considering plans as far-reaching as Oregon's. Most, however, are tinkering with the existing system to guarantee health care access for at least some of their uninsured citizens. Finding the money to do so is a constant concern. The Robert Wood Johnson Foundation, a private philanthropic group, is funding several small demonstration projects in various states. State lawmakers say that federal money would be helpful as well. Representative Jim McDermott (D-Wash.) has sponsored a bill to provide $25 million in federal planning grants for states to provide low-cost insurance for the working poor. So far, no action has been taken on the bill.

For the time being, then, it looks as though the most innovative solutions to the problem of providing universal access will occur in the states. "My guess is that in the next decade we will have some kind of universal insurance entitlement," says Jeffrey Merrill, vice president at the Robert Wood Johnson Foundation. "How it looks may vary from state to state; some may be public, some may be private, some traditional, some radical."

Many argue that the health care system will never come close to serving everyone until nationwide, comprehensive reform is undertaken. The successes and failures of these state initiatives, however, may provide a roadmap for any far-reaching changes of the health care system in the United States.

17 CASE STUDY: STATE HEALTH CARE PROGRAMS

HAWAII'S MANDATED HEALTH PLAN: The Point

John C. Lewin, M.D.

John C. Lewin is Director of the Hawaii State Department of Health.

Points to Consider:

1. What is meant by a "mandated" health care plan?

2. How is Hawaii's system different from proposed "national" plans?

3. Who are the "gap group" and how are they covered by Hawaii's mandated scheme?

4. How is Hawaii's mandated system paid for?

Excerpted from testimony by John C. Lewin before the House Committee on the Budget, June 19, 1991.

The Prepaid Health Care Act is the nation's first and only state mandated benefits plan. Virtually all employers are required to provide health insurance to their employees.

Hawaii is often thought of as a tropical paradise. Unknown is the fact that we have one of the best basic health systems in the nation. Our system delivers high-quality care for low cost, despite our otherwise high cost of living. Early intervention and outpatient treatment are emphasized, but Hawaii also enjoys high-tech tertiary care programs as advanced as that of any state or nation. This system has resulted in very low infant mortality rates, along with the lowest death rates from such chronic illnesses as cancer and heart disease. This happened despite the troubling health statistics of our Hawaiian and part Hawaiian residents.

The key, I would hold, to our success is our state's longstanding commitment to ensuring that basic health care is available to all our people and to its innovative health care community. This community has experimented with ideas like short hospital stays, outpatient surgery, and preventive health programs, long before they became the norm on the mainland United States.

Likewise, our state has implemented a mandated employer benefits program, the only one of its kind in the nation. And we have recently put on the road our subsidized insurance program (the State Health Insurance Program) to offer coverage to those left in the gap between these other programs. These programs are not panaceas for the national crisis of the uninsured—and we don't take them as such. But, neither are they inapplicable to the people of California, South Dakota, New Hampshire, or any other state. We have something of value to share, and look forward to working with our partner states.

Prepaid Health Care Act

Let us first start off by exploring a few basics about the current structures in Hawaii's system. The Prepaid Health Care Act was adopted in 1974 to provide health insurance and medical protection insurance for most employees in the State. The Act is administered by the State's Department of Labor and Industrial Relations. This measure was passed in 1974, after many years of study and policy development. The measure was passed in a time of moderate unemployment in an environment

"OH, HIM... HE HAS ONE OF THOSE BARE-BONES HEALTH INSURANCE POLICIES."

of already strong employment-based health care coverage. Effects on unemployment have been negligible: in fact, over the last 16 years, our unemployment rate has fallen to the lowest in the nation. (I make no claims about a cause-effect relationship in this regard. But this seems to at least cast some doubt on assertions that such mandates will cause unemployment).

The Prepaid Health Care Act is the nation's first and only state mandated benefits plan. Virtually all employers are required to provide health insurance to their employees. Dependent coverage is optional. Costs are shared in this program. The employee pays up to 1.5 percent of monthly wages up to half the premium cost. The employer provides the balance. Employers may provide benefits as outlined in the Act on a self-insured basis, but are still subject to the requirements that those services be provided.

Community Rating

By requiring virtually all employers to provide insurance, Prepaid Health Care has permitted health care contractors to provide health insurance rates for small employers comparable to those enjoyed by large employers. This has happened because all small businesses now form a large risk pool. Adverse risks are part of the overall pool, which eliminated the need for insurance companies to individually rate employers.

The results have been extremely positive. Small business can purchase insurance at reasonable rates. Employees are covered with health insurance. Insurance companies cut administrative costs and can market to a large pool of businesses. Prepaid Health Care has provided a uniformly level field for competition. Responsible small businesses who provide health insurance are not at a competitive disadvantage relative to those who do not.

Medicaid

Hawaii's Medicaid Program services over 72,000 persons with a budget of about $220 million. It is administered by the State's Department of Human Services.

Hawaii provides Medicaid to both the categorically needy and medically needy persons. Elderly and disabled persons with income up to 100 percent of the poverty level, and children under age six with income up to 133 percent of the poverty level are covered. We have chosen the option to provide coverage for pregnant women and infants with income up to the maximum allowed by statute (185 percent of poverty). We have also implemented the "presumptive eligibility" provision for pregnant women to encourage early prenatal care.

The Gap Group (Uninsured people)

The effects of these programs, particularly Prepaid Health Care, is evident. In 1971, Hawaii had 17 percent of its population in the gap group (uninsured) and was similar in this regard to California and East Coast states. The implementation of Prepaid Health Care brought about a dramatic drop in those figures in several surveys conducted at the time.

People at risk in the gap group are largely made up of those who, for one reason or another, lack access to Prepaid Health Care. As found in a 1988 survey, the unemployed make up over 30 percent of Oahu's uninsured. This is likely also true of the neighbor islands. Dependents of low-income workers, particularly children, are another major gap group. Part-time workers, excluded from Prepaid Health Care, are another population at risk. Neighbor island residents, immigrants, seasonal workers and students are also at risk, although they are not formally excluded from Prepaid Health Care.

110

Our Ship Is In!

To meet the needs of this gap group, the State Health Insurance Program (SHIP) was implemented. The program provides universal access to basic health care services to all of Hawaii's people by building upon Hawaii's Prepaid Health Care Act and Medicaid.

SHIP has been created to subsidize affordable health care coverage, encourage usage of private insurance and Medicaid and to discourage shift to SHIP from private coverage. SHIP is thus designated as a partnership between government, individuals and families, and the private sector. Through SHIP, government subsidizes insurance coverage for those unable to pay. Insurance companies provide the coverage and the already existing health care providers deliver direct care.

Benefits of SHIP are heavily weighted toward preventive and primary care, with health appraisals and related tests, well-baby and well-child care coverage and accidents fully covered. To be eligible for SHIP, you must be a Hawaii resident with gross income less than 300 percent of the poverty level. SHIP eligibility is subject to enrollment and fiscal limits and must be renewed on a yearly basis.

A Novel Experiment

Rather than attempting to create a national health insurance or national health delivery system, Hawaii strongly recommends a "national health policy of benefits for all citizens to be implemented and organized by the fifty states." Cost should be shared by both federal and state governments.

As for our own specific recommendations, Hawaii envisions implementing the nation's first seamless universal health system as a national demonstration project. We believe that we have a plan which would build on present strengths, correct weaknesses, and increase efficiency while reducing costs. Ours is a private sector model of managed competition; promoting incentives, consumer choice, private practice, and private insurance, with heavy emphasis on primary care.

Some of our recommendations would alter current federal policies or programs which unduly inhibit state capacity for experimentation. We propose such flexibility, mindful of the memorable words of Justice Brandeis: "To stop experimentation on things social and economic is a grave responsibility. Denial of the right to experiment may be fraught with serious consequences to the nation. It is one of the happy incidents of the federal system that a single courageous state may, if its citizens choose, serve as a laboratory; and try novel social and economic experiments without risk to the rest of the country."

18 CASE STUDY: STATE HEALTH CARE PROGRAMS

MANDATED HEALTH PLANS:
The Counterpoint

National Restaurant Association

The National Restaurant Association represents the views of the food service industry and small businesses in their opposition to health insurance mandates. The Association presented a background paper in testimony before Congress and supports a cost-control solution to the health care crisis.

Points to Consider:

1. Why are mandates unfair to small businesses?

2. What is the greatest obstacle to small businesses in providing health insurance? Explain.

3. Who would suffer the most under a mandated system?

4. How would cost controls be better than mandates?

Excerpted from testimony submitted by the National Restaurant Association before the U.S. Senate Committee on Finance, April 9 and 16, 1991.

Restaurants and other small businesses are especially sensitive to the cost increases imposed by mandates.

When the U.S. spends nearly 12 percent of its GNP on health care, and at the same time an estimated 31 million Americans remain uninsured, the warning is obvious: something is seriously wrong in the U.S. health care system.

As the leading trade association for the food service industry, the National Restaurant Association is concerned about gaps in health care coverage and about runaway health care costs. Food service, which employs about seven percent of the U.S. workforce, is an industry dominated by small business, those often least able to provide health insurance. National Restaurant Association research shows that most food service operators would like to offer health insurance to employees—and generally do so, as profits and size increase. However, operators report that the single greatest obstacle to providing insurance is cost.

Food service operators are working with Congress to find ways to reduce health care costs so employers who want to provide health insurance can do so. Neither the broad-brush approach of a government mandate nor a tax on employers who already cannot afford coverage are realistic solutions to the problems of uninsured workers. Forcing all American businesses to provide health care benefits, regardless of the cost, will in the long run only hurt those Congress is trying to help.

Costs Are Up

A recent National Restaurant Association survey shows that the cost for food service employer's share of health insurance premiums rose a minimum of 23 percent between 1987 and 1989. Some operators experienced increases averaging 60 percent over that two-year period.

How have operators held up under these financial strains? In addition to bearing the cost of increased premiums, more companies are finding it necessary to require hourly employees to shoulder some of the financial load for health insurance coverage.

Small Businesses Suffer

In late 1989, the National Restaurant Association polled smaller restaurants who do not provide insurance. Among small firms with annual sales of less than $500,000, almost three-quarters said they did not provide health insurance because premiums were too high. Nearly two-thirds of this group said their company was not profitable enough.

Even in light of these problems, however, food service operators want to provide insurance. Restaurant owners know that in order to attract and keep a loyal and stable workforce, they must offer good benefits. Health insurance is generally one of the first benefits they offer.

Statistics prove the point. As sales volume increases for a food service operation, the likelihood of providing health care coverage for both hourly and salaried employees increases. Association research shows that 30 percent of food service companies with annual sales under $500,000 provide insurance for both hourly and salaried employees; the percentage climbs to 72 percent for companies with sales between $1 and $5 million a year, and 87 percent for companies with yearly sales over $10 million. Left to voluntary measures, employers will take action.

A Mandate Is No Solution

The food service industry employs large numbers of young, inexperienced and part-time workers, many of whom would otherwise be without jobs.

Many of these employees are only marginally attached to the workforce. They may be students with part-time jobs, or second earners who are not interested in full-time work. Employees like these are often looking for part-time or seasonal work that will bring in some extra cash. The food service industry has provided this opportunity for millions of American workers, reducing the nation's unemployment rate while at the same time answering these employees' needs for flexible work that give them the job experience that can boost them further up the employment ladder.

Yet most National Restaurant Association members could not afford to provide these employees with the array of benefits a mandate would require. For small independent restaurants already faced with high payroll costs, the additional expense of providing comprehensive health benefits to all employees—without regard to their productivity—is simply prohibitive. It is hard enough for restaurants to provide even a barebones health plan. The likely result of a government mandated health plan would be fewer jobs for these marginally attached workers.

Moreover, a mandate removes the choice that is the hallmark of a free market system and forces adult employees to participate in their employer's health care plan regardless of whether they want, need, or can afford the coverage.

Cutting Costs

The National Restaurant Association recommends that lawmakers direct their attention to removing the barriers that discourage employers from providing health insurance. Food service operators ask Congress to take the following six steps:

1. Develop cost-containment measures, both long- and short-term. Establish physician practice guidelines, find ways to eliminate unnecessary procedures and revise medical malpractice laws to reduce liability insurance costs for physicians.

2. Scrutinize the practices of insurers. The National Restaurant Association questions the role of the insurance industry in accepting employers' insurance premiums for years and years and then hiking premiums dramatically or cancelling insurance completely when workers file claims.

The government should examine these practices, as well as take action to prohibit insurers from issuing blanket denials of coverage to certain small businesses and occupations that insurers arbitrarily deem risky.

3. Provide favorable tax treatment for employers who provide benefits and for individuals who purchase health insurance.

4. Examine continuation benefits. Hearings were never held on a 1985 law that requires employers to offer former employees and their dependents the opportunity to continue participating in group health plans. Also, making health insurance more expensive for those employers who are already giving their best effort to offer health benefits is leading to less coverage, not more.

5. Eliminate state mandates. There are currently over 800 state mandates that drive up the cost of health insurance, requiring even basic insurance policies to cover such services as acupuncturists, and chiropractors. By stopping these mandates and allowing employers to offer a less expensive, no-frill health benefits package, the federal government would allow businesses to provide employees with at least some type of coverage.

Food service operators want to provide health insurance for their workers. For employers and employees alike, however, the biggest deterrent to health care coverage is cost. The National Restaurant Association asks Congress to craft incentive-based solutions that will allow businesses to continue to provide health care coverage for employees and remove the barriers that prevent so many of them from doing so.

19 CASE STUDY: STATE HEALTH CARE PROGRAMS

MINNESOTA'S HEALTHRIGHT ACT: Points and Counterpoints

Arthur L. Caplan and Steven Miles
vs.
A. Stuart Hanson

Arthur L. Caplan teaches in the Center for Biomedical Ethics at the University of Minnesota. Steven Miles is a physician in the Hennepin County Medical Center in Minneapolis. They wrote this article originally for The Baltimore Sun. *A. Stuart Hanson is a practicing physician. His comments were taken from congressional testimony he gave in his capacity as President of the Minnesota Medical Association (MMA).*

Points to Consider:

1. How does "HealthRight" provide health care coverage?

2. Who pays for "HealthRight"?

3. How is Minnesota's plan different from that of Oregon and other state initiatives?

4. Which approach elsewhere in this chapter best describes the Minnesota plan?

Arthur L. Caplan and Steven Miles, "Nation Can Learn from Minnesota's HealthRight Act", Minneapolis **Star-Tribune,** April 30, 1992 and from testimony by A. Stuart Hanson, M.D. before the House Energy Commerce Committee, April 3, 1992.

THE POINT

Arthur L. Caplan and Steven Miles

If there is anything Americans agree on it is that their health care system is a mess. Yet, people ranging from White House officials to health economists are just as certain that a cure is years away. They are wrong. Minnesota has come up with a practical plan to fix its health care system.

HealthRight

[In April, 1992, Minnesota] Governor Arne Carlson signed into law legislation known as HealthRight. Legislators on the left and the right were able to break through the gridlock that has developed in national health policy by realizing that the control of health care costs and provision of access to affordable insurance are not incompatible goals. The opposite is true. Movement became possible in Minnesota with the political awareness that allowed liberal and conservatives to see that the only way to increase access to health care is by making changes in the system that will contain costs.

HealthRight moves to contain costs by instituting some simple, long overdue reforms. It mandates that private insurance companies doing business in the state sell basic coverage that does not exclude the sick and disabled, or charge women and older people exorbitant premiums. This means cheaper insurance will be available to every citizen.

Lowering Costs

The legislation bans conflict-of-interest ownership arrangements and self-referrals by health care providers. This lowers costs by cutting down on unnecessary tests and procedures. The law creates minimal practice guidelines for physicians, which will lower the stratospheric costs of malpractice insurance and defensive medicine. And a state commission will regulate the purchase of new technologies and large capital investments by hospitals, as well as set targets for what the state is willing to pay for those Minnesotans who get their health care through state programs.

These reforms will cut costs, freeing more money to help subsidize insurance for the uninsured.

Revenues

Additional revenues for subsidizing insurance for the uninsured are generated by raising the cigarette tax a nickel a pack, adding a two percent surcharge on all hospital, doctor and dentists' bills, and imposing a one percent tax on all HMOs and nonprofit insurers' bills. Medicaid and Medicare charges are exempt from these new excise taxes.

The doctors and hospitals hate the new taxes. But HealthRight deliberately uses taxes on providers rather than money from general revenues to force greater efficiency in the health care industry. By imposing a tax on providers and establishing real reforms in the existing system, the money can be found to put affordable insurance within reach of the 400,000 children and adults in Minnesota who have no coverage.

Not a Handout

Under the provisions of HealthRight, all Minnesotans who do not qualify for Medicaid or Medicare will be able to buy health insurance with a subsidy pegged to their income. HealthRight is not a handout. Each person must carry some of the burden of the cost. A family of three earning roughly $10,000 a year can buy a basic package of health services for $8 a month. The state will pay $300. If that same family earns $30,000 a year or more, it can still buy HealthRight insurance, but it pays the full $300 monthly premium.

HealthRight does not address every health care need. Outpatient services, prenatal care, immunizations, eyeglasses and short hospital stays form the core of the coverage available under the subsidized insurance scheme. Prevention gets much more attention than catastrophic illness or injury. But by emphasizing prevention and health maintenance, HealthRight lowers the odds that Minnesotans are going to find themselves in a hospital or nursing home.

Unlike Oregon, the only other state to try health care reform seriously, Minnesota has constructed a program that provides access to the uninsured without demanding rationed care for the poor. Other states and Congress should take a cue from Minnesota. The only way to provide affordable, quality health care to all Americans is by swallowing the politically bitter medicine of cost containment.

Editor's Note:

Due to recent court decisions and several federal regulations, states like Minnesota are currently facing roadblocks to health care reform. Federal laws governing uniformity in pension and benefit rules could force plans such as Minnesota's HealthRight to falter. Such federal laws may hamper those states that are leading the way toward improving the nation's health care system.

THE COUNTERPOINT

A. Stuart Hanson, M.D.

The Minnesota Medical Association (MMA) has been very active in working to improve access to health care — particularly for the uninsured. Last year, we organized the Medical Benefits Task Force to define basic medical care. But despite our support for the goals of HealthRight, we are deeply concerned that some provisions in the bill will actually reduce access to health care. I would like to make three points about this bill as it is currently written.

First, HealthRight is a dramatic move away from the competitive model of health care delivery that has made Minnesota a worldwide leader. Right now Minnesotans receive higher quality health care services at lower costs than residents of any other state. A New York health firm, Milliman and Robertson, evaluated health care costs in the nation's 400 largest cities. Los Angeles ranked number one, and the Twin Cities was way down on the list as 238th. This is quite an accomplishment — especially since the Twin Cities is the thirteenth largest metropolitan area in the country. Health care in Minnesota's rural areas is even less expensive. At the same time that we keep costs down, Minnesota ranks among the top healthiest states in national studies conducted by Northwestern National Life Insurance. It has kept quality up and costs down.

But HealthRight would make a dramatic change from our competitive model to the use of strong government regulation to control costs. HealthRight would set an "annual limit on the rate of growth for public and private spending on health care services." This is meant to reduce unnecessary care. But it won't work. Minnesota doesn't have the amount of unnecessary care that is reported on the national level. We have already eliminated it. So HealthRight would limit spending on necessary care.

The bill leaves several troubling questions unanswered. How will these spending limits will be imposed? What will happen when the spending limit is exceeded and there are people waiting in line for operations? Do we cut them off? Canadians, who can't get a CAT scan or a coronary bypass operation without waiting for months, come down to our border cities and see Minnesota physicians. I hope that Minnesotans won't have to drive to Wisconsin or Iowa to get medical care. It will be very hard for the state to predict how much money will be needed in a given year for medical care. It's even harder to imagine how the state will begin to control private health care spending. Will limits apply only to state residents or to the people from other states and other countries who come to the Mayo Clinic?

We have serious doubts that vesting enormous powers in a state commission with limited medical expertise will mean more efficient and better health care for Minnesotans. Our fear is that it will lead to rationing.

We don't deny that our current health care system is a form of economic rationing because it excludes the uninsured. Our common goal is to make sure all Minnesotans get the health care they need regardless of how much money they make. I think we can do that without turning to another kind of rationing. If the state sets spending caps for private and public health care and limits the medical technology that is available to our patients, health care may be rationed for everyone.

Finally, the Minnesota Medical Association (MMA) is concerned that HealthRight will have a devastating effect on rural Minnesota. The 2% sales tax on health services will cripple Minnesota's ability to recruit new physicians in rural areas. Recruitment is already hard. A 1990 MMA survey found that 75% of rural physicians were actively trying to recruit physicians to join their practice and 80% were having difficulty. HealthRight may make recruitment impossible. Many rural physicians are approaching retirement age. We may not be able to replace them.

The HealthRight program may cost even more than legislators estimate, and so far the state does not appear able to pay the real cost of providing health care. Minnesota's difficulty in finding enough money to pay for its existing programs is already making it hard for people in rural Minnesota to get the medical care they need.

The problem is that Medical Assistance reimbursement often doesn't even cover the physicians's cost of overhead such as rent, payroll and equipment. It costs a physician money to treat every Medical Assistance patient. This means that practices with a high percentage of Medical Assistance patients are struggling to continue. In rural Minnesota, the median percentage of Medical Assistance patients is three times higher than in a metropolitan practice.

The MMA believes that everyone in the state should share the cost of helping people who can't afford health insurance. HealthRight should be funded by a broad-based tax such as an income tax. The Minnesota Medical Association urges legislators to amend HealthRight so that it will improve rather than reduce access to health care in Minnesota.

READING THE DAILY NEWSPAPER

One of the best sources for obtaining current information on important social and political issues affecting our society is the daily newspaper. The skill to read with insight and understanding involves the ability to know where to look and how to "skim" the headlines for articles of interest. The best place to begin is the front page and first section as well as the opinion/editorial pages (op/ed). Other good sources include the sections on the economy and special feature sections that are usually popular in the Sunday editions. Be sure not to overlook the sections that deal with local and regional issues as they often contain stories of global concern that are happening in your own community.

Guidelines

Using newspapers from home or from your school or local library, skim the headlines and locate articles that deal with health care and medical ethics. Be sure to check the Sunday edition for special sections on health issues. With heated debate taking place today on health care reform, the headlines and editorials are a good source of information for current legislative action on this subject.

1. Try to locate several articles dealing with current efforts to reform our health care system.

2. Do any of these articles agree or disagree with the readings in Chapter Three?

3. Below are listed the major categories of health care reform now being discussed in the U.S. Describe each approach in two or three sentences; then match each reading in Chapter Three with the appropriate category below:

    A. Universal (National) Single-Payer Health Care

    B. Free Market Method

    C. Mandated Health Care

D. Expanding existing programs in the private and public sector.

Be sure to indicate if a combination of approaches is suggested.

4. Choose the method you agree with most. Using the appropriate reading(s) and any newspaper clippings you have located, be prepared to defend your position in a class discussion. Pay particular attention to current health care legislation and political proposals.

5. Locate a current article that presents a first-hand account of someone's personal difficulty in obtaining proper health care. How does his/her story illustrate a particular point made in this book? Explain.

CHAPTER 4

RATIONING HEALTH CARE & THE OREGON EXPERIMENT

20 RATIONING HEALTH CARE & THE OREGON EXPERIMENT

HEALTH CARE RATIONING IS ETHICAL

Daniel Callahan

Daniel Callahan is director of the Hastings Center and author of two books on the allocation of health care and resources: "Setting Limits: Medical Goals in an Aging Society", *and* "What Kind of Life: The Limits of Medical Progress".

Points to Consider:

1. Why is health care costing so much for the elderly?

2. How do the young suffer from this?

3. How should we redefine old age?

4. What is meant by a "natural life span"?

Daniel Callahan, "Limiting Health Care for the Old", **The Nation,** August 15/22, 1987.
Copyright © 1987 by Daniel Callahan. Reprinted by permission of Simon and Shuster.

A longer life does not guarantee a better life.

In 1980, people over age 65 – 11 percent of the population – accounted for 29 percent of the total American health care expenditures of $219.4 billion. By 1986, the elderly accounted for 31 percent of the total expenditures of $450 billion. Annual Medicare costs are projected to rise from $75 billion in 1986 to $114 billion by the year 2000, and that is in current, not inflated dollars.

Escalating Costs

Is it sensible, in the face of the rapidly increasing burden of health care costs for the elderly, to press forward with new and expensive ways of extending their lives? Is it possible even to hope to control costs while simultaneously supporting innovative research which generates new ways to spend money? Those are now unavoidable questions. The fastest growing age group in the United States is comprised of those over age 65, increasing at a rate of about 10 percent every two years. By the year 2040, it has been projected, the elderly will represent 21 percent of the population and consume 45 percent of all health care expenditures. How can costs of that magnitude be borne?

Anyone who works closely with the elderly recognizes that the present Medicare and Medicaid programs are grossly inadequate in meeting their real and full needs. The system fails most notably in providing decent long-term care and medical care that does not constitute a heavy out-of-pocket drain. Members of minority groups and single or widowed women are particularly disadvantaged. How will it be possible, then, to provide the growing number of elderly with even present levels of care, much less to rid the system of its inadequacies and inequities, and at the same time add expensive new technologies?

The straight answer is that it will be impossible to do all those things and, worse still, it may be harmful even to try. Other cultures have believed that aging should be accepted, and that it should be in part a time of preparation for death. Our culture seems increasingly to dispute that view, preferring instead, it often seems, to think of aging as hardly more than another disease, to be fought and rejected. Which view is correct?

Redefining Old Age

Let me interject my own opinion. The future goal of medical science should be to improve the quality of old peoples' lives, not to lengthen them. In its longstanding ambition to forestall death, medicine has reached its last frontier in the care of the aged. Of course children and young adults still die of maladies that are open to potential cure, but the highest proportion of the dying (70 percent) are over 65. If death is ever to be humbled, that is where endless work remains to be done. But however tempting the challenge of that last frontier, medicine should restrain itself. To do otherwise would mean neglecting the needs of other age groups and of the old themselves.

Our culture has worked hard to redefine old age as a time of liberation, not decline, a time of travel, of new ventures in education and self-discovery, of the ever-accessible tennis court or golf course and of delightfully periodic but thankfully brief visits from well-behaved grandchildren. That is, to be sure, an idealized picture. But it arouses hopes that spur medicine to wage an aggressive war against the infirmities of old age. As we have seen, the costs of such a war would be prohibitive.

Natural Life Span

There is a plausible alternative: a fresh vision of what it means to live a decently long and adequate life. (What might be called a "natural life span".) Earlier generations accepted the idea that there was a natural life span — the biblical norm of three score and ten captures that notion (even though in fact that was a much longer life span than was typical in ancient times.) It is an idea well worth reconsidering and would provide us with a meaningful and realizable goal. Modern medicine and biology have done much, however, to wean us from that kind of thinking. They have insinuated the belief that the average life span is not a natural fact at all, but instead one that is strictly dependent on the state of medical knowledge and skill. And there is much to that belief as a statistical fact: the average life expectancy continues to increase, with no end in sight.

But that is not what I think we ought to mean by a natural life span. We need a notion of a full life that is based on some deeper understanding of human needs and possibilities, not on the state of medical technology or its potential. We should think of a natural life span as the achievement of a life that is sufficiently long to take advantage of those opportunities life typically offers and that we ordinarily regard as its prime benefits — loving and "living", raising a family, engaging in work that is satisfying, reading, thinking, cherishing our friends and families. People differ on what might be a full natural life span; my view is that it can be achieved by the late 70s or early 80s.

A longer life does not guarantee a better life. No matter how

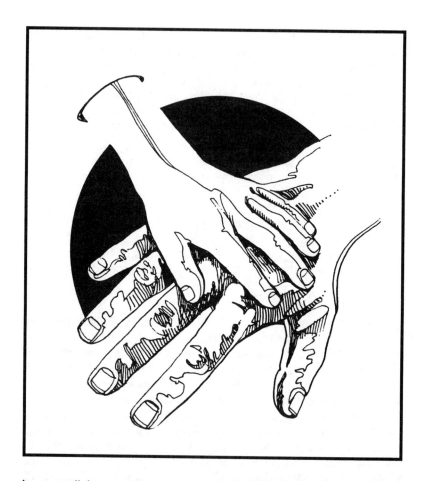

long medicine enables people to live, death at any time—at age 90 or 100 or 110—would frustrate some possibility, some as-yet-unrealized goal. The easily preventable death of a young child is an outrage. Death from an incurable disease of someone in the prime of young adulthood is a tragedy. But death at an old age, after a long and full life, is simply sad, a part of life itself.

As it confronts aging, medicine should have as its specific goals the averting of premature death, that is, death prior to the completion of a natural life span, and thereafter, the relief of suffering. It should pursue those goals so that the elderly can finish out their years with as little needless pain as possible—and with as much vitality as can be generated in contributing to the welfare of younger age groups and to the community of which they are a part. Above all, the elderly need to have a sense of the meaning and significance of their stage in life, one that is not dependent on economic productivity or physical vigor.

Bottomless Spending

The indefinite extension of life combined with an insatiable ambition to improve the health of the elderly is a recipe for bottomless spending. It fails to put health in its proper place as only one among many human goods. It fails to accept aging and death as part of the human condition. It fails to present to younger generations a model of wise stewardship.

How might we devise a plan to limit the costs of health care for the aged under public programs that is fair, humane and sensitive to their special requirements and dignity? Let me suggest three principles. First, government has a duty, based on our collective social obligations, to help people live out a natural life span but not to help medically extend life beyond that point. Second, government is obliged to develop under its research subsidies, and to pay for under its entitlement programs, only the kind and degree of life-extending technology necessary for medicine to achieve and serve the aim of a natural life span. Third, beyond the point of a natural life span, government should provide only the means necessary for the relief of suffering, not those for life-extending technology.

The elderly will not be served by a belief that only a lack of resources, and better financing mechanisms or political power stands between them and the limitations of their bodies. The good of younger age groups will not be served by inspiring in them a desire to live to an old age that maintains the vitality of youth indefinitely, as if old age were nothing but a sign that medicine has failed in its mission. The future of our society will not be served by allowing expenditures on health care for the elderly to escalate endlessly and uncontrollably, fueled by the false belief that anything less is to deny the elderly their dignity.

21   RATIONING HEALTH CARE & THE OREGON EXPERIMENT

HEALTH CARE RATIONING IS NOT ETHICAL

Amitai Etzioni

Amitai Etzioni is a visiting professor at the Harvard Business School and author of the book "The Moral Dimension".

Points to Consider:

1. Why are the elderly an easy target?

2. What is the "slippery slope" theory? Explain.

3. What is intergenerational equity? Why is it an issue?

4. What ways are there to allocate health care resources?

Amitai Etzioni, "Spare the Old, Save the Young", **The Nation**, June 11, 1988. © 1988 **The Nation** Company, Inc. Reprinted with permission.

It is a dubious sociological achievement to foment conflict between the generations.

In the coming years, Daniel Callahan's call to ration health care for the elderly, put forth in his book *Setting Limits*, is likely to have a growing appeal.

The Slippery Slope

In order to free up economic resources for the young, Callahan offers the older generation a deal: trade quantity for quality; the elderly should not be given life-extending services but better years while alive. Instead of the relentless attempt to push death to an older age, Callahan would stop all development of life-extending technologies and prohibit the use of ones at hand for those who outlive their "natural" life span, say, the age of 75. At the same time, the old would be granted more palliative medicine (e.g., pain killers) and more nursing home and home-health care, to make their natural years more comfortable.

Callahan's call to break an existing ethical taboo and replace it with another, raises the problem known among ethicists and sociologists as the "slippery slope". Once the precept that one should do "all one can" to avert death is given up, and attempts are made to fix a specific age for a full life, why stop there? If, for instance, the American economy experiences hard times in the 1990s, should the "maximum" age be reduced to 72, 65 — or lower? And should the care for other so-called unproductive groups be cut off, even if they are younger? Should countries that are economically worse off than the United States set their limit, say, at 55?

Withholding Technology

Callahan suggests turning off life-extending technology for all those above a certain age, even if they could recover their full human capacity if treated. It is instructive to look at the list of technologies he would withhold: mechanical ventilation, artificial resuscitation, antibiotics and artificial nutrition and hydration. Note that while several of these are used to maintain brain-dead bodies, they are also used for individuals who are temporarily incapacitated but able to recover fully; indeed, they are used to save young lives, say, after a car accident. There is no way to stop the development of such new technologies and the improvement of existing ones without depriving the young of benefit as well.

Cartoon by Thompson, **State Journal Register**

One may say that this is Callahan's particular list; other lists may well be drawn. But any of them would start us down the slope. Any significant foray into deliberately withholding medical care for those who can recover does raise the question, once society has embarked on such a slope, where will it stop?

The Elderly

Those opposed to Callahan, and the other advocates of limiting care to the old, but who also favor extending the frontier of life, must answer the question, where will the resources come from? One answer is found in the realization that defining people as old at the age of 65 is outdated. That age limit was set generations ago, before changes in life styles and medicines extended not only life but also the number and quality of productive years. One might recognize that many of the "elderly" can contribute to society not merely by providing love, companionship and wisdom to the young, but also by continuing to work, in the traditional sense of the term. Indeed, many already work in the underground economy because of the large penalty—a cut in Social Security benefits—exacted from them if they hold a job "on the books".

Allowing elderly people to retain their Social Security benefits while working, typically part-time, would immediately raise significant tax revenues, dramatically change the much-feared dependency-to-dependent ratio, provide a much-needed source of child-care workers and increase contributions to Social Security.

Equity

Policies that seek to promote intergenerational equity must be assessed as to how they deal with another matter of equity: that between the poor and the rich. A policy that would stop federal support for certain kinds of care, as Callahan and others propose, would halt treatment for the aged, poor, the near-poor and even the less well-off segment of the middle class (although for the latter at a later point), while the rich would continue to buy all the care they wanted. Callahan's suggestion that a consensus of doctors would stop certain kinds of care for all elderly people is quite impractical; for it to work, most if not all doctors would have to agree to participate. Even if this somehow happened, the rich would buy their services overseas either by going there or by importing the services. There is little enough we can do to significantly enhance economic equality. Do we want to increase inequalities that already exist by completely eliminating access to major categories of health care services for those who cannot afford to pay for them?

There are other major targets to consider within health care, as well as other areas, which seem, at least by some criteria, much more inviting than terminating care to those above a certain age. Within the medical sector, for example, why not stop all interventions for which there is no hard evidence that they are beneficial? Say, public financing of psychotherapy and coronary bypass operations? Why not take the $2 billion or so from plastic surgery dedicated to face lifts, reducing behinds and the like? Or require that all burials be done by low-cost cremations rather than by using high-cost coffins?

Minor Cause

The high-technology medicine Callahan targets for savings is actually a minor cause of the increase in health care costs for the elderly or for anyone—about four percent. A major factor is the very high standard of living American doctors have, compared to those of many other nations. Indeed, many doctors tell interviewers that they love their work and would do it for half their current income as long as the incomes of their fellow practitioners were also cut. Another important area of saving is the exorbitant profits made by the nondoctor owners of dialysis units and nursing homes. If we dare ask how many years of life are enough, should we not also be able to ask how much profit is "enough"? This profit, by the way, is largely set not by the market but by public policy.

The answer is in the eye of the beholder. There are no objective criteria that can be used between the races or between the genders.

22 RATIONING HEALTH CARE & THE OREGON EXPERIMENT

OREGON'S PLAN HURTS WOMEN AND CHILDREN

James W. Malone

James W. Malone is a Roman Catholic Bishop and Chairman of the Domestic Policy Committee for the United States Catholic Council.

Points to Consider:

1. Why is the Oregon Plan inequitable? Explain.

2. How does the plan exclude basic health care?

3. How does Oregon's plan violate federal policies?

4. Why will women and children suffer from this plan? Give several examples.

Excerpted from testimony by Bishop James W. Malone before the U.S. House Subcommittee on Health and the Environment of the Committee on Energy and Commerce, September 16, 1991.

The Oregon Plan is inequitable in concept and cruelly life-threatening for the most vulnerable of the state's children.

Good intentions cannot justify Oregon's proposed intentional rationing of health care for the poor. The proposal is inequitable in concept, arbitrary and capricious in effect, violative of the purposes of the Medicaid program, and cruelly life-threatening for the most vulnerable of the state's children.

Inequitable in Concept

The Oregon proposal to fund only certain health services from a list developed by the state is a radically new rationing concept. Unlike the rationing familiar to us in moments of national crisis, this plan is to be applied not to all citizens of Oregon, but only to its poor. While in future years the listings may be used to establish minimum coverage for those with private insurance, Oregon now plans to use them as the maximum coverage for the poor under the Medicaid program. It is only the poor and most vulnerable—those eligible for Medicaid—whose health care is to be rationed. For more than one hundred and sixty thousand poor women and children currently covered by Medicaid, the plan would take away medical coverage for over 120 medical conditions, almost one-fifth of the treatments in Oregon's medical listings.

This fundamental inequity is exacerbated by the proposed double standard within the Medicaid eligible population. The Oregon plan would initially exempt tens of thousands of Medicaid recipients who are aged, blind, or disabled from the rationing scheme. Their medical care actually constitutes more than two-thirds of the state's total Medicaid bill and is the fastest growing part, while care for children on Medicaid comprises less than 15 percent of Oregon's Medicaid budget.

Basic Care

Despite its own commission recommendation, the Oregon Legislature did not agree to provide "basic health care". The legislature approved only a partial listing of covered services and excluded eight "essential" health services—including seven in the "acute fatal" and "chronic fatal" categories—and more than fifty "very important" health services. Even within the conceptual structure of the Oregon plan, its failure to fund basic health care is arbitrary and capricious. It is a product of political and fiscal

Map by Ron Swanson

considerations, not good medicine, justice, or sound social policy.

In coming years, the Oregon legislature may exclude more and more "essential" and "very important" health services and further erode "basic health care" for Medicaid participants, primarily women and children.

Use of the medical listings threatens traditional medicine's focus on the care and cure of individual patients. It would shift us from patient-centered to procedure-driven medical practice. It would take away individualized medical decisions about what is good or even life-saving for a particular patient and substitute in its place a generalized determination of what seems to be good for some average population.

The listings thus also threaten to change the traditional relationship between physicians and patients, at least for poor patients. Many doctors already refuse to participate in Medicaid because of underfunding of services. These radical and pervasive changes in medical practice could seriously aggravate the current shortage of doctors and other providers in Medicaid by substituting the political judgments underlying the listings for the medical judgments of individual physicians. The losers, again, would be poor women and children.

Finally, the arbitrariness of the state proposal is highlighted by the Legislature's decision to increase subsidies for abortion, funded only by state monies under this plan but expanded now to additional thousands of persons, in lieu of funding life-saving health care for the poor in Oregon.

Violating the Law

The purpose of the Medicaid law is to enable the states to furnish "medical assistance on behalf of families with dependent children and of aged, blind, or disabled individuals, whose income and resources are insufficient to meet the costs of necessary medical services. . . ." The clear purpose is to provide medical coverage to the two groups singled out since the Depression for special government care and protection: poor families with children and the aged, blind, or disabled. In the interim, Congress has adopted a number of mandates and options focused on expansion of coverage for both groups. These culminated in the 1990 law that will insure coverage of all poor children by the year 2001.

Reverse Policy

Oregon's proposal would now reverse that long-standing federal policy. On the one hand Oregon protects the politically more powerful group of elders and persons with disabilities from drastic benefit cuts while, on the other, it subjects the more vulnerable group of its poorest women and children to the state's untested plan. Exposing the poorest women and children to the broad dangers inherent in this untried plan cannot be justified.

Discarding Care

Secondly, not only does the proposed plan not provide the basic health care recommended by Oregon's own commission, but it totally discards the provision of medically necessary care and services required under the Medicaid law and protected for years by both Congress and the courts.

Children Lose Out

Thirdly, Oregon's poor children have little to gain and much to lose under the proposal. The Medicaid amendments of 1989 and 1990 have entitled all poor children to all medically necessary care and services. All states, including Oregon, must extend coverage to all poor children under age nineteen. Younger children have the most costly health needs, the most to gain by congressional mandates, and the most to lose in Oregon's scheme. In fact, almost every pregnant woman and child under six with family incomes under 133 percent of the poverty line and every poor Oregon child under nine loses essential and very important, even life-saving, medical care under the plan.

The Poor Suffer

Furthermore, while Oregon protests that its plan is intended to benefit poor women and children, it proposes to eliminate the medically needy program for pregnant women and children under age 18. This provision was designed by Congress specifically to assist women and children who have medical problems causing excessive medical costs. Oregon would strip them of this medical coverage.

Finally, the radically experimental and untested nature of the Oregon proposal threatens the health, well-being, and lives of hundreds of thousands of poor Oregonians, its poorest women and children and thousands of others. Both ethics and public policy dictate that experimentation involving human subjects, such as research under the Medicaid program, be subject to strict controls. In each such case, the government must exercise extreme care to analyze whether the risks involved in the experiment are outweighed by the benefits to those involved.

The government must also establish safeguards to protect people from experiments by the Oregon proposal.

Guinea Pigs

In this case, the vast majority of the subjects of the Oregon plan will be children incapable of voluntary consent to the experiment. A humane medical ethic suggests that children should not be subjected to an experimental plan unless the research might benefit them as individuals. Before allowing states to subject children to such experimentation, the federal government then has a particularly heavy legal and ethical responsibility to protect their health and lives.

While expanding abortion services, Oregon's proposal directly terminates access to care for 120 health services of a hundred and sixty thousand poor women and children currently covered by its Medicaid program. This is more than just an experiment in health care financing or an alternation in the funding structure of the state program. In fact, the plan could result in federally sanctioned medical neglect leading to the deaths of poor women and children. One such example occurs in the case of extremely premature and low birthweight newborns, whose survival has been given low priority in the state's listings. In the case of these young children, individualized medical and ethical decisions should be made by appropriate family members and professionals. Instead, Oregon proposes an automatic, cost-based, and formula-triggered denial of funding for treatment and thus sentences these children to almost certain death.

In view of the numerous moral, ethical, and policy imperatives against the kind of experimentation proposed for the poor of Oregon, the Roman Catholic bishops of this nation must oppose the Oregon experiment.

23 RATIONING HEALTH CARE & THE OREGON EXPERIMENT

OREGON'S PLAN BENEFITS WOMEN AND CHILDREN

Mary Ann Curry

Mary Ann Curry is a member of the Oregon Healthy Mothers and Healthy Babies Coalition.

Points to Consider:

1. Who primarily benefits from the Oregon Plan?

2. How are benefits and services actually increased? Explain.

3. How is preventive care affected by the plan?

4. Why is Oregon's plan better than expanding Medicaid only?

Excerpted from testimony by Mary Ann Curry before the U.S. House Subcommittee on Health and the Environment of the Committee on Energy and Commerce, September 16, 1991.

***The Oregon Plan is good for our most vulnerable
women and children, those living under the poverty
line.***

It is my strong conviction that the Oregon Plan is good for
women and children. Furthermore, it is a good plan for our most
vulnerable women and children, those living under the poverty
line.

Before I describe why I believe it is a good plan for women
and children, it is important that we all appreciate the fact that
the Oregon Plan creates a serious rub with some of our most
deeply held American values. It may be this rub that is at the
root of some of the opposition. First, the Plan defines health
care from a societal perspective rather than from an individual
perspective. Second, the Plan makes our current system of
rationing explicit instead of implicit. This is a particularly irritating
rub for those who believe (or want to believe) rationing does not
exist. Currently, federally funded health care is rationed
according to income, family structure, and age. Finally, it is
viewed as a threat to the hard-won federally mandated programs
for women and children that advocates such as the Children's
Defense Fund (CDF) have achieved. The rub here is with the
values that organizations such as CDF hold, unfortunately values
not shared by all Americans.

Unwarranted Criticism

Two major criticisms of why the Plan is not good for women
and children are: (1) it discriminates against our most vulnerable
women and children, and (2) it simply reduces benefits to
low-income women and children. I believe the Oregon Plan
achieves exactly the opposite effect. It improves access to
health care for the most vulnerable women and children—those
living under the Federal Poverty Line (FPL). As you know, it is
estimated that nearly half of the 120,000 newly eligible will be
women and children. This means that children over eight won't
have to wait until their earache develops into a severe ear
infection (and an expensive trip to the Emergency Room) to be
treated. And it means that low-income single women and women
whose children are living with them will have access to health
care.

Deprivation

Working in the homeless shelter exposed me to a level of

Source: **The People**

deprivation I didn't know existed. The women who came in for exams they hadn't had for years were some of the most vulnerable women I have ever seen. Their general health condition was appalling.

The shelter also exposed me to the harsh reality of what it is like for a woman to lose custody of her children. There is not only emotional pain for these women, but also the sudden loss of access to health care and other benefits. It was not unusual for these women to become pregnant again. Most smoked heavily, many were chemically addicted, and nearly all were depressed. They spent most of the time surviving: finding a meal or a place to live. The Oregon Plan obviously won't solve all of these problems, but it will provide access to health care for many of these women at one of the most critical times in their lives and the lives of their future children: the time before and during conception.

Services Decreased

I'd like to focus my remarks on the second major criticism, that the Plan simply reduces benefits to low-income women and children. I believe the Plan does not decrease benefits, but instead provides the most beneficial services. This has been at the heart of much of the criticism: that the Plan is "taking away" valuable services.

Beneficial Services

Under the Oregon Plan, priority is given to those services that are believed to be of the most value to society and the individual, and are essential to basic health. One of those services is the opportunity to have an appointment with a provider, and an accurate diagnosis, as all appropriate screening and diagnostic services are covered. This means women could have a mammogram and pap smear, two of the most cost-beneficial screening procedures available. It would mean that school-age children could have a health exam before starting school and be screened for hearing, vision, and learning problems.

One of the most beneficial services of the Plan is preventive care that will be integrated into all visits with providers. Look at what would be available to children between seven and 12, for whom the leading causes of death are motor vehicle crashes and accidents. When they have an appointment with their provider, a component of that care would include counseling regarding safety belts; smoke detectors; storage of firearms, drugs, chemicals, and matches; and bicycle safety helmets. Similarly, women between 40-64, for whom the leading causes of death are lung, breast, colon, and reproductive cancer, would be counseled about tobacco use, diet, and breast self-exam. These are services not currently covered by Medicaid.

Women and Children

Another criticism is that the current funding level does not provide for an adequate benefits package. I don't believe this is true, especially for women and children. In fact, the Oregon Health Action Campaign summarized the benefits as "better than most folks get with private insurance". All of the major diseases women experience, including physical and sexual abuse, are covered. Likewise, all major diseases of children are covered, in addition to the preventive counseling aimed at reducing the leading causes of death: accidents, suicide, and homicide. Furthermore, dental care is covered, which is significant, as currently only one-third of American children receive dental care.

I strongly believe the Oregon Plan is good for women and children. It is unquestionably better for those 120,000 persons who would be newly eligible. Furthermore, I believe it is a more beneficial set of services than those currently provided. What has been "taken away" are the least effective, least beneficial services.

I believe it is completely amoral that as a society we do not provide universal access to maternity care for all women and health care for all children. However, that is not our current reality. In addition, I am under no illusion that providing universal access to maternity care will make a significant improvement in the health of our women and children as long as their basic needs for housing, food, education and safety remain unmet.

The Federal Poverty Line (FPL)

Improving the access to primary health care that reimburses for preventive health should have a significant positive effect on the birth outcomes of childbearing women living under the FPL. Nonpregnant women can be helped to adopt healthier lifestyles, like stopping smoking, before becoming pregnant, with the potential for reducing maternal and fetal complications. Because of increased access to family planning, more women will have the opportunity to plan their pregnancies, a key factor in predicting pregnancy outcome. In addition, women with existing medical problems, such as diabetes, can be adequately treated before becoming pregnant.

Under our current system, we try to cram all of this into the time we have with women during pregnancy and the six weeks after birth. However, some conditions, such as tape worms, cannot be treated during pregnancy, and there are simply some limits to what can be accomplished in a short period of time. If we know a woman will not be eligible for Medicaid after her six week postpartum visit, we are often faced with the dilemma of how much to do before her eligibility expires.

I believe the Oregon plan is good for women and children. It improves access to health care for our most vulnerable women and children, those living under the Poverty Line. It offers them a package of services that will be of the most benefit to them and to society.

RECOGNIZING AUTHOR'S POINT OF VIEW

This activity may be used as an individualized study guide for students in libraries and resource centers or as a discussion catalyst in small group and classroom discussions.

The capacity to recognize an author's point of view is an essential reading skill. Good readers make clear distinctions between descriptive articles that relate factual information and articles that express a point of view. Think about the readings in Chapter Four. Are these readings essentially descriptive articles that relate factual information or articles that attempt to persuade through editorial commentary and analysis?

Guidelines

1. Read through the following source descriptions. Choose one of the source descriptions that best describes each reading in Chapter Four.

    Source Descriptions

    a. Essentially an article that relates factual information

    b. Essentially an article that expresses editorial points of view

    c. Both of the above

    d. None of the above

2. After careful consideration, pick out one reading in Chapter Four that you agree with the most. Be prepared to explain the reasons for your choice in a general class discussion.

3. Choose one of the source descriptions above that best describes the other readings in this book.

4. Read through the following statements and mark each factual statement with an **(F)**; mark each statement that expresses an opinion with an **(O)**. Any statement you are unsure of, mark with a **(?)**.

_____ By 1986, the elderly accounted for 31 percent of total health care expenditures.

_____ Members of minority groups and single or widowed women are particularly disadvantaged.

_____ A longer life does not guarantee a better life.

_____ The elderly make an especially easy target because they take a big slice of health care resources.

_____ Rationing health care is unfair.

_____ Oregon's rationing plan is good for poor children.

_____ All states, including Oregon, must extend coverage to all poor children under age 19.

_____ In Oregon, women with existing medical problems, such as diabetes, can be treated before becoming pregnant.

_____ A universal system of health care is needed which would eliminate the need for any rationing of health care.

_____ Rationing health care has worked in Oregon.

_____ All health care schemes are rationed in one way or another.

_____ The future of our society will not be served by allowing more health care for the elderly at the expense of the young.

CHAPTER 5

GLOBAL HEALTH CARE PERSPECTIVES

24 GLOBAL HEALTH CARE PERSPECTIVES

GLOBAL HEALTH CARE OVERVIEW

Janet L. Shikles

Janet L. Shikles is the director of Health Care Financing and Policy Issues for the General Accounting Office. She directed the preparation of a report on health care systems in France, Germany and Japan. Excerpts from her report are included in the following reading. All industrialized nations except the United States and South Africa have national comprehensive health care programs similar to those in France, Germany and Japan. Health care in South Africa, the (former) Soviet Union and the United Kingdom are covered separately by an editor's overview. Sweden's system is described by excerpts from a Swedish Embassy report. High quality health care in most poor and developing nations is usually available only for wealthy people and the ruling elite. The vast majority of people in poor nations are normally left outside the health care system. Cuba and Bolivia, two poor nations that have just made progress in extending health care to the poor, are also described in the reading that follows.

Points to Consider:

1. How does health care cost and access in Western Europe compare to that of the U.S.?

2. Has the national approach worked in Sweden? In Britain?

3. Why is health care in Cuba and Bolivia considered a model for the Third World?

4. What is the condition of health care in South Africa and Russia?

Janet L. Shikles, "Health Care Spending: The Experience of France, Germany and Japan", U.S. General Accounting Office Report, November 1991.

France, Germany, and Japan: A Mandated Approach [1]

France, Germany, and Japan achieve near-universal health insurance coverage within health care systems that share three main traits with the U.S. system: (1) medical care is provided by private physicians and by both private and public hospitals, and patients have free choice of physician; (2) most people receive health insurance coverage through their workplace; and (3) health insurance is provided by multiple third-party insurers.

Per capita spending on health care ranged in 1989 from $1,035 (U.S. dollars) in Japan, to $1,232 in West Germany and $1,274 in France. The U.S. spent $2,354 per person for health care that same year.

These similarities to the U.S. system coexist with several notable differences that follow from the far-reaching regulations used to guarantee coverage. First, insurers—who are predominantly non-profit—are required to provide minimum coverage that includes a wide range of health care benefits. Second, insurance enrollment is compulsory (with minor exceptions) for all residents, and they have little or no choice of insurers. Third, workplace-based insurance is financed not by premiums that reflect each individual group's expected costs of care, but largely by employer and employee payroll contributions that reflect the average cost of a larger cross section of the population.

In addition to mandating insurance coverage, all three countries standardize reimbursement rates for almost all physicians and hospitals and set ceilings (price controls) on these rates. Virtually all payers must, when reimbursing providers, abide by the standardized rates. Reimbursement rates are not set by the government unilaterally, but emerge from formal or informal negotiations between physicians, hospitals, third-party payers, and (in France and Japan) the government.

Private Medicine and Patient Choice

In France, Germany, and Japan, as in the United States, patients generally can choose their own physician; outpatient services are provided by private physicians; and inpatient care is provided in both private and public hospitals.

---

[1] Excerpted from a **U.S. Government Accounting Office** report titled "Health Care Spending Control: The Experience of France, Germany, and Japan", November 1991.

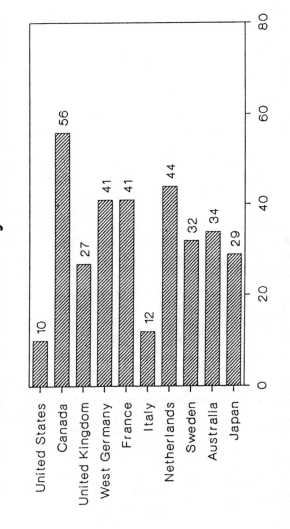

Percent of Citizens Who Think
Their Nation's Health System Works Well

United States	10
Canada	56
United Kingdom	27
West Germany	41
France	41
Italy	12
Netherlands	44
Sweden	32
Australia	34
Japan	29

Source: U.S. Senate Committee on Finance, April 9, 1991

Physicians who provide outpatient services are paid on a fee-for-service basis—as are most U.S. physicians. (Unlike in the United States, however, physicians who deliver inpatient care are often employed by a hospital on a salaried basis.)

Health Insurance

Each country guarantees virtually all their residents health insurance that offers a broad minimum level of benefits. Near-universal coverage is achieved by making enrollment for health insurance compulsory, with few exceptions, and virtually automatic.

Mandated (Required) Benefits

The mandated package of health benefits covers a wide range of services. Benefits generally include coverage for physician services, hospital care, laboratory tests, prescription drugs, and some dental and optical care.

Payroll-Based

Workplace-based insurance in France, Germany and Japan is largely financed by mandatory payroll contributions from both employees and employers. In contrast to private insurance financing in the United States, which generally reflects each individual group's expected costs of care, these mandatory contributions reflect the average cost of a larger cross section of the population than typically used by U.S. insurers in calculating premiums. (In France and Japan, payroll-based financing is supplemented by subsidies from general tax revenues.)

Other members of the population—those who are not employed or have a special employment status—receive health benefits in one of two ways. The first method is illustrated by France and Germany, where the sickness funds that insure most employees also cover retirees and unemployed people. France also has national sickness funds for self-employed persons and for agricultural workers. Germany requires self-employed persons below an income threshold to join one of the work place-based sickness funds. By contrast, in Japan, members of these groups are generally covered through a separate program of public insurance known as National Health Insurance.

Health Care Spending

Each country has national procedures for setting limits on health care spending and for determining standardized reimbursement rates for providers. Generally, a government agency or other authorized body sets broad targets for all or some components of health care spending. The targets may serve as guidelines or they may be binding. National laws also require that payers reimburse providers according to rates that are, for the most part, uniform; a given service is usually reimbursed at the same rate, regardless of payer.

Each country also has a formal process for settling payment rates for physicians and hospitals. The health care system's major stakeholders—third-party payers, physicians and hospitals, and (in France and Japan) the government—participate in this rate-setting process. In France and Germany, the rates are set in formal negotiations. In Japan, they are set by the government in consultation with a body that represents insurers and health care providers.

Controlling Cost

Seeking to moderate the rise in health care spending, all three countries have imposed direct controls on health care prices and overall spending. These controls are comprehensive—applying to the entire health care industry or to a major health care sector. Each country sets limits on overall health spending as national goals, but only France and Germany have added policies with teeth to achieve compliance with the limits.

Sweden: Local Government at Work [2]

Health and medical care is regarded as an important part of the Swedish welfare system. Its fundamental principle is that all citizens are entitled to good health and equal access to health and medical care, regardless of where they live and their economic circumstances. In line with this principle, health and medical care is seen as a public sector responsibility which is supported by a national health insurance system and by other social welfare services.

The national system organizes both physician services and hospital care and is funded by general taxes. All Swedish citizens are guaranteed access to these services which are free. Responsibility for health and medical care, both inpatient and outpatient, has hitherto been a duty of the 23 county councils and three large municipalities (Goteborg, Malmo, Gotland). These units, with populations ranging from some 60,000 to 1.5

[2] Excerpted from a fact sheet published by the **Embassy of Sweden**, titled "Health and Medical Care In Sweden", October 1991.

million, also operate the public dental service and services for the mentally handicapped. Responsibility for social welfare services rests primarily with the municipalities, which are 284 in number (286 from January 1, 1992) and have populations ranging from about 5,000 to 700,000.

Private health care exists on a limited scale only—about five percent of physicians work full-time in private practice. The corresponding figure for private dentists, however, is more than 50 percent. A limited number of private medical care institutions chiefly provide long-term nursing care. There are few signs of an increase of interest in private health care.

Britain and Canada: The National Approach [3]

Britain and Canada have approached health care with government-run universal schemes that provide cradle-to-grave services for their citizens. Financed through general taxation, these national health plans enable patients to receive free services and to choose both their own hospitals and doctors. The programs pay a salary to physicians for services rendered, and all hospitals charges are covered as well.

In Britain, the National Health Service employs over 25,000 general practitioners who work at the local level in group practices (GPs). Britons register with a local GP, and the government then pays a fee to that GP according to the number of patients it registers. In addition, Britain employs more than 14,000 dentists and operates over 2000 hospitals.

Life expectancies in the U.K. are similar to those of the U.S. at about one-third the cost. Critics of the British System cite a backlog of patients waiting for relatively simple operations, and hospitals overstaffed with salaried physicians and trade-union employees who lack incentive and productivity.

Canada's health care system is also paid for through taxation and operated by a public insurance scheme in each of the provinces. Administrative costs are much less than in the U.S., making it a popular model of reform for some Americans. Critics claim such a system would not work in the U.S. A more complete debate on the Canadian Health Care System can be found in the readings that follow.

---

[3] Information gathered from an article by Tom Hamburger titled "Condition Critical: Canada's Solution", **Star Tribune**, September 29, 1991, and by Norman Macrae titled "The Good Health Guide", **National Review**, December 16, 1991.

Cuba: Model for the Third World [4]

*(Editor's Note: The following article describes a state-run approach to health care in a poor Marxist nation, written by the **People's Daily World**, a pro-communist and pro-Castro weekly newspaper.)*

Cuba's health care system is one of the proudest achievements of its Revolution. The World Health Organization (WHO) and other United Nations agencies point to the Cuban system, which makes health services ranging from primary care to the most complex procedure freely available to city dweller or rural resident alike, as a model for developing countries.

With more than 39,000 practicing physicians, Cuba's health statistics rival those of the most advanced countries. Infant mortality has declined from 38 deaths/1,000 live births in 1959 to less than 11 in 1991. Life expectancy is approaching that of the U.S. and is still improving. Diphtheria, malaria, polio, whooping cough and other "silent killers" of Third World children have practically been eliminated.

Clinics dot the countryside and are open day and night to all citizens. Doctors and nurses often make house calls to older or very ill residents. Personnel attend conferences and lectures to keep up on the latest medical technology. Patients with serious conditions are admitted to a more advanced clinic or hospital. The country has developed heart disease and cancer therapies and conducts basic biological research, and specialized training in diagnostic technique.

The U.S. blockade has put severe strains on the Cuban health care system, hitting with particular force at the special needs of children. In a speech to the U.N. General Assembly, Cuban Ambassador Ricardo Alarcon de Quensada cited several items of medical equipment used in children's hospitals that were no longer available to his country.

Bolivia: Health Care for the Poor [5]

(Editor's Note: The following article describes attempts to solve health care problems in a poor nation with a capitalist

[4] Excerpted from an article titled "Cuban Health Care System Model for the Third World", **People's Daily World**, January 25, 1992.

[5] Excerpted from an article by Baird Straughan titled "Self-financing Health Project Brings Quality Care to Bolivia's Poor," **Front Lines,** February 1992.

economy. It was described in **Front Lines**, *a monthly news letter published by the U. S. Department of State.*)

Before the PROSALUD clinic came to El Pailon—a village on the outskirts of Santa Cruz, Bolivia, in 1985, the community had never had a doctor or nurse. El Pailon's primitive health post was run by an elderly veteran of the Bolivian army. Today the 3,000 people of El Pailon are served by a health clinic with a medical staff provided through PROSALUD, a self-financing health-care organization begun with funding from USAID/Bolivia.

PROSALUD is one of the very few primary health care organizations in the world that serves the poor and is, nevertheless, self-financing. PROSALUD's central office in Santa Cruz administers 16 clinics that serve 125,000 people in the poor rural and semi-urban areas around the tropical city. The growing population had strained the public health system beyond its limits. Today, in health centers where the attention previously was sporadic, PROSALUD offers poor patients round-the-clock care.

PROSALUD clinic staff provide free preventive services like vaccinations or well-baby examinations. They charge for curative services at rates equivalent to those of the public health service. Commonly prescribed medicines are available at the in-house pharmacy. What impresses health care practitioners most is that, while expanding, PROSALUD has been able to finance itself. The quality of its care and its financial management have attracted requests for assistance from health organizations around Latin America.

"It's not the case that the working poor can't pay," says PROSALUD National Executive Director Dr. Carlos Cuellar. "After all, how do they pay for a ride on the bus? It's that you have to give them attractive, personal medical service for which they're willing to pay. If you go to a public clinic and are treated badly, you won't want to pay either."

"In PROSALUD, we try to synthesize the best from both the public and private sectors, creating a new type of community organization among the poor, showing them that privatization doesn't mean lining the pockets of the rich. This is a new model in which a private initiative can help satisfy community needs."

Russia and South Africa: Health Care in Decay [6]

Both South Africa and the former Soviet Union are suffering from national health care systems that are at severe risk. In the former Soviet Republics, city hospitals are critically short of life-essential drugs, new syringes, x-ray machines, antibiotics, aspirin, cotton, bandages, and other basic medical supplies. They are dark, grimy places where doctors are overworked and sanitation is often neglected. In rural areas the situation is much worse. The former Soviet Health Ministry reported in 1990 that half of the hospitals and clinics had no sewer systems, 80 percent had no hot water, and 17 percent had no piped water at all.

The Universal system under the former Soviet government has fallen into chaos with doctors in the public sector being paid less than most bus drivers. Even though there are clinics with advanced and innovative care—such as those for eye surgery— the rewards in medicine are dwindling for ordinary doctors. Many disgruntled doctors, nurses and hospital employees have gone on strike.

In South Africa, besieged by Third World illnesses and rising urbanization, the situation is also deteriorating. The government's long-term goal is an affordable and accessible health care system for all citizens, but currently doctors are overworked, equipment is outdated and academic hospitals in the cities are overcrowded. Most of these patients could be treated at local clinics or mid-level facilities. The private sector provides some 34,000 hospital beds for about 20 percent of the population, while the public sector provides only 89,000 beds for 80 percent of the population.

[6] Information gathered from the following articles: Steven Erlanger, "Cuts Gut Russian Health Care", **New York Times**, May 1992; Eleanor Randolph, "Soviet Hospitals Besieged by Filth, Shortage of Drugs", **Washington Post**, November 1991; and Mari Hudson, "Sick Image of South Africa's Health Services", **Die Burger**, Capetown, December 12, 1990.

GLOBAL HEALTH CARE
PERSPECTIVES

CANADA'S HEALTH CARE SYSTEM IS SOUND

Perrin Beatty

Perrin Beatty is the Minister of Health and Welfare in Canada. This reading is taken from an article by Mr. Beatty distributed by the Canadian Embassy.

Points to Consider:

1. How are the provinces involved in the Canadian Health Care System?

2. Who pays for the Canadian system? Who is covered?

3. How do access and costs compare with the current U.S. system?

4. Why are costs lower in Canada?

Perrin Beatty, "Health Care in Canada", **Canadian Embassy Circular**, March 1991.

Canada's system has succeeded in providing high-quality care to all Canadians.

Canada has a taxpayer-financed, comprehensive health care system that covers hospital and doctor's services for all residents, regardless of ability to pay. All Canadians have access to well-trained doctors and well-equipped hospitals.

Because the provinces have constitutional authority for health care delivery, the system is made up of interlocking provincial health plans. The federal government sets basic standards and contributes financially to the operation of the provincial plans. It also provides health services directly to natives, the military and other special groups.

How the System Works

When Canadians need medical care, they go to the doctor, clinic or hospital of their choice and present their enrollment card (issued to all residents of a province). Doctors bill the province; patients do not pay directly for medical services and they are not required to fill out forms. There are no deductibles or co-payments.

Most doctors are in private practice and are paid on a fee-for-service basis under a fee schedule negotiated between the provincial medical association and the provincial government. About 95 percent of the hospitals in Canada are non-profit and are operated by voluntary organizations, municipalities or other agencies. Hospital administrators have complete control of the day-to-day allocation of resources as long as they stay within the annual operating budgets they negotiate with the province. They are accountable to local boards of trustees, not to the provincial or federal bureaucracy.

Evolution of Universal Insurance

It took almost 40 years for Canada's health care system to evolve into its present form. After the Second World War, the federal government urged the provinces to establish health insurance plans that would cover most Canadians, and offered to share in the costs. Although no agreement was reached, some of the provinces went ahead without federal funding. Saskatchewan was the first province to establish, in 1947, public, universal hospital insurance. By 1949, British Columbia had a similar program and Alberta and Newfoundland had hospital plans that provided partial coverage.

In 1957, Parliament passed legislation to allow the federal government to share in the costs of provincial hospital insurance plans that met minimum eligibility and coverage standards. By 1961, all 10 provinces and the two territories had public insurance plans that provided comprehensive coverage for hospital care, covering 95 percent of the population.

Saskatchewan again pioneered in providing insurance for outpatient medical services, in 1962. The federal government passed medical care legislation in 1966, and by 1972, all of the provincial plans had been extended to include doctor's services.

In 1980, a royal commission was formed to review health care in Canada. Its chairman was retired Supreme Court Justice Emmett Hall, who had led an earlier royal commission that recommended nationwide medical insurance in 1964. The commission reported that health care in Canada ranked among the best in the world, but it warned that extra billing by doctors was creating a two-tiered system that threatened the accessibility of care.

The Canada Health Act was passed in 1984 to respond to fears of financial barriers to access and to reaffirm the federal government's commitment to a universal health care insurance system. The act sets out the basic standards the provinces must meet to receive federal funding. It discourages provincial user charges and extra billing by providing for a dollar-for-dollar reduction in the federal contribution.

Provincial Flexibility

As long as they meet the criteria specified in the Canada Health Act, the provinces have considerable flexibility in the organization and delivery of health services. The provincial plans offer a range of supplementary benefits, such as prescription drugs for the elderly and dental care for children, which vary from province to province. (Employee benefit plans cover some other services, such as optometry and physical therapy.) Although user fees have been eliminated for acute hospital care under the Canada Health Act, provinces are allowed to charge patients for meals and accommodations in chronic care facilities.

Funding

In 1989, health care spending in Canada totalled an estimated C$56.1 billion (US$47.4 billion) Funds for the provincial plans may be supplemented by sales taxes, taxes levied on employers or premiums paid by individuals. Only Alberta and British

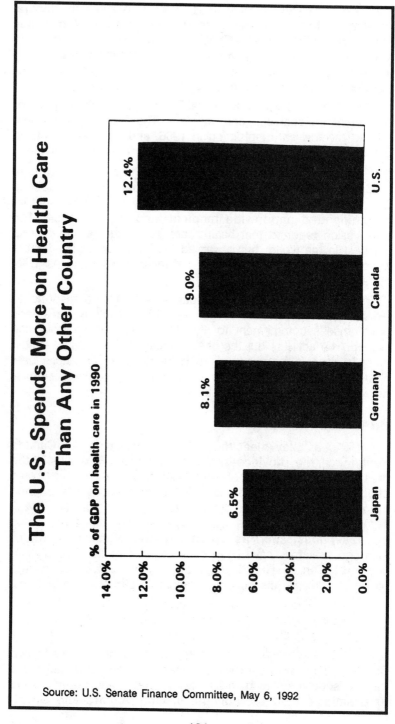

The U.S. Spends More on Health Care Than Any Other Country

% of GDP on health care in 1990

Country	% of GDP
Japan	6.5%
Germany	8.1%
Canada	9.0%
U.S.	12.4%

Source: U.S. Senate Finance Committee, May 6, 1992

Columbia collect premiums. The premiums are not rated by risk in either province, and prior payment of a premium is not a condition of eligibility for treatment.

Until 1977, the federal contribution was linked to the cost of health services, roughly matching provincial expenditures. The federal contribution now takes the form of block grants and tax transfers to the provinces. A separate annual federal grant is made to each province toward the costs of extended care provided outside hospitals. The federal contribution is financed through consolidated revenues (personal and corporate income taxes, excise taxes, import duties, etc.).

Cost Control

Significantly lower administrative costs are a major factor in keeping costs down in Canada. Administration accounts for about 2.5 percent of total health costs in Canada, compared to 8.5 percent in the U.S. Under the Canadian system, with a single insurer for each provincial plan (compared to 1,500 private insurers in the U.S.), the costs of marketing, estimating risk status, setting premiums and deciding who should be covered are avoided.

Administrative costs are also reduced for hospitals and doctors; since they bill the province rather than patients directly, they don't need to verify coverage or complete the paperwork required by multiple private insurers, and they don't have to cope with problems of double-billing, uninsured patients and collection of unpaid debts.

Another factor which reduces doctors' expenses in Canada is the relatively low cost of malpractice insurance premiums. Most doctors are insured through membership in the Canadian Medical Protective Association, a non-profit organization.

The provinces have considerable power to limit health care spending. A hospital's operating costs must be paid out of the annual budget it negotiates with the provincial ministry of health. The province must approve in advance a hospital's capital expenditures, for new facilities, major renovations or new equipment, and may refuse to pay the operating costs of facilities or equipment acquired without its approval, even if the acquisition was privately financed. This degree of control results in higher utilization rates for hospital beds and high-technology equipment in Canada.

Any increase in payments for doctors' or nurses' services is set by negotiations between the province and the provincial associations. For doctors, the medical association usually decides how the increase will be divided among the medical specialties.

Although the system is efficient, it faces continued pressure to contain costs which are escalating rapidly. Canada has the second highest level of per capita spending on health care in the world, and health care is already the largest component of every provincial budget.

Support for Canada's System

Canadians consider health care to be a basic right, and they value their health care system highly. All three major political parties support the system. Canadian business was initially skeptical that government could administer health care more efficiently than the private sector. Today, however, business supports the health care program, not only because it has proved to be efficient but because the burden of paying for it is spread across society.

Perhaps more surprisingly, the Canadian Medical Association also supports the program, and a recent survey of doctors found that nearly two-thirds were satisfied or very satisfied with the practice of medical insurance in Canada. They like it because they are guaranteed payment, and while the government provides the financing, it is reluctant to interfere with their professional autonomy.

Occasional disagreements have arisen between the provincial governments and health professionals, particularly over fees and billing. When public insurance for medical services was first proposed in Saskatchewan in 1962, doctors closed their offices in protest for 23 days. Doctors in Ontario also went on strike in 1986, when the province outlawed extra billing.

The Canada Health Act requires that the provinces provide doctors with "reasonable compensation". Doctors' income is in the top one percentile of all Canadians. According to Revenue Canada, the average net income (after expenses, before tax) of self-employed Canadian doctors in 1988 was US$86,928. Incomes vary by province; for example, the 1988 average in Newfoundland was $86,522, while in Ontario it was $99,927.

The medical profession remains an attractive one in Canada—the number of doctors per capita has grown steadily since the introduction of medical care insurance, and there is even some concern that Canada has an oversupply. There are more than 57,000 doctors now practicing in Canada, about one for every 450 people.

Criticism and Response

Critics of Canada's health care system contend that it involves "rationing" and results in crowded hospitals, outdated equipment and long waiting lists.

Supporters respond that medical care is rationed in Canada only on the basis of the needs of the patients. While waiting periods do at times exist in some regions for certain diagnostic and elective surgical procedures, patients who are in need of immediate treatment are admitted without delay. The province has the option of increasing hospital resources if it determines that lack of hospital beds or waiting lists are affecting the quality of care.

Expensive high-tech equipment is distributed among a region's hospitals to avoid unnecessary duplication of services. Cost-control processes do tend to delay the introduction of new technology until its effectiveness has been thoroughly assessed. To aid hospitals in determining whether acquisition of technology will enhance patient care, the federal and provincial governments have established a Coordinating Office for Health Technology Assessment.

Canada's health care system is based on consensus, and such issues as funding, shortages or inadequacies are resolved through public and political debate. Although the debate has been at times divisive, it has resulted in a system that adapts to stresses as they arise. Most importantly, Canada's system has succeeded in providing high-quality care to all Canadians. One measure of its success is the robust health of Canadians. Their average life expectancy of 77.2 years (compared to 75.4 for Americans) is among the highest in the world, while the infant mortality rate of seven per 1,000 live births (compared to 11 in the U.S.) is one of the lowest.

CANADA'S HEALTH CARE SYSTEM IS FLAWED

Michael Walker

Michael Walker is executive director of the Fraser Institute in Vancouver, British Columbia, Canada, and has written extensively on health care issues in Canada.

Points to Consider:

1. Why haven't demand and price risen more sharply in Canada?

2. How are costs controlled by the Canadian system?

3. Why are there problems with waiting lists in Canada? Explain.

4. How is health care rationed in Canada?

5. Why does the author feel a Canadian-type system would not work in the U.S.?

Being insured in Canada is no guarantee that you will receive medical care when you need it—and waiting sometimes means death.

It is not entirely correct to refer to "the Canadian health care system," for it actually includes 11 separate provincial and federal health care programs operating under the umbrella of the National Health Act. The federal government provides a significant but declining fraction of health care funding. It also tries to ensure national standards, portability of coverage, and elimination of co-insurance payments or user fees by penalizing provincial governments that break the rules.

Patients may pay extra for semi-private and private hospital rooms since the basic service covers only ward accommodation. Patients may also pay for services that aren't covered by the hospital plan, including elective plastic surgery or out patient physical therapy. They may not, however, pay a doctor anything more than the government's fee for covered services, and the doctor may not accept any extra payment.

(This prohibition extends to hospital services or surgical procedures. Canadian patients may not "jump the queue" by paying directly for procedures in short supply. Patients of other nationalities may, however, get access to Canadian health care faster than Canadians by paying the full cost themselves. The argument used to justify this practice is that letting foreigners pay cash generates more money for the health care system and hence, enables more Canadians to be treated.)

Cost Comparisons

So why does Canada do things so much more cheaply than the United States? The most significant fraction of the difference, according to the *New England Journal of Medicine,* is in the costs of administering the two systems. To administer the U.S. system takes 1.23 percent of the Gross Domestic Product (GDP), compared to a mere 0.1 percent for the Canadian system.

Add to that the fact that Canadian physicians are protected from unlimited liability by a Supreme Court-imposed ceiling on pain-suffering damages and the further fact that Canadians have a younger population, and considerably more than half of the difference is accounted for. What's more, notes Victor Fuchs, a Stanford University researcher and noted health care authority, Canadian doctors charge smaller fees. Casual observation of the salaries offered by American recruiters at nursing job fairs in Canada indicates that other health care personnel also earn more in the United States.

But even all these factors do not entirely account for the difference. There is, after all, the pesky matter of the demand for health care. Since 1971, Canadians have had universal access to the medical system—with fees of any kind forbidden by law. Health care is, in other words, a free good. And, as a Royal Commission of Enquiry determined in 1976, "the demand for health care appears to be unlimited." In such a system, we would expect demand for care to skyrocket, taking costs along with it.

A Set Budget

Oddly enough, this hasn't happened. The reason is simple, though not obvious: Canada doesn't control the unit cost of health care—the cost, for instance, of an appendectomy—but the total cost. Each provincial government sets a health care budget for the year and pays each hospital accordingly. Although nominally independent, hospitals depend entirely on these politically determined budgets for their revenue.

No matter how much demand there may be, the hospitals usually do not receive any additional payment. Any operating deficit must be made up in the next fiscal year. To meet these restraints, hospitals limit the total number of complicated surgeries—cardiac bypasses, hip replacements—they can do in a particular budgetary period. They also reduce the number of available beds to bring their total operating expenses down to the budgeted figure. This practice, on a system-wide basis, amounts to rationing.

The provincial governments also control hospitals' capital budgets—thereby limiting the acquisition of new technologies. And the governments allocate money separately for such special procedures as cardiac bypass surgery, rationing them as well. As a result, there are many fewer open-heart surgery sites and organ transplant facilities per capita in Canada than in the United States.

Although physicians are paid on a fee-for-service basis, with fees negotiated collectively, they, too, are limited to a fixed amount of total billing. If total billings exceed the budget for a certain period, each physician's payments in the next period are reduced to make up the difference.

"ACCORDING TO THIS STUDY, WE SPEND LESS ON HEALTH CARE THAN THE U.S. BECAUSE WE DON'T HAVE NEARLY AS MUCH PAPERWORK...."

Cartoon by Trever, **Albuquerque Journal**

Take a Number

So the answer to the question, "How do they do it in Canada?", is that they do not do it. The total cost of health care is controlled by arbitrarily limiting the number of procedures of certain types, by limiting access to technology and diagnostic machinery, and by compensating physicians so that they are discouraged from responding to the demands of their patients. There are measurable consequences of this supply limitation in the form of lines or waiting lists for surgery.

As the celebrated case of Stanley Roberts, former president of the Canadian Chamber of Commerce, makes clear, being insured in Canada is no guarantee that you will receive medical care when you need it—even if the required treatment is a fairly standard procedure. Roberts was admitted to Burnaby General Hospital near Vancouver with neurological symptoms—memory loss, speech impediment, headache. The cause, it was determined, was either a tumor or an abscess.

If an abscess, it needed immediate treatment, since these can fulminate and kill the patient relatively quickly. If a tumor, while potentially just as deadly if malignant, there would be more time to treat it. Roberts was placed on the waiting list for neurosurgery to have a biopsy or other definitive test of his malady. It turned out to be an abscess — a fact determined by an autopsy after Roberts had died. For Stan Roberts, a personal friend and a man who had done much for Canada in many capacities during his life, the waiting list for diagnostic surgery proved to be too long. Until recently, such tragic stories accounted for most of our knowledge of Canadian waiting lists; there was little hard information available. But the Fraser Institute has just completed a five-province study of patient waiting.

In all, 333 physicians representing 10 different specialties were surveyed — 20 percent of the total number of practitioners in each of the fields of specialization. Physicians were asked to indicate how many patients they had waiting for procedures of different kinds and how long people were waiting before they got the service they needed.

These survey responses constitute a unique source of information, because comprehensive surveys of this kind have not been conducted by others and, in particular, no waiting list measurements are published by provincial governments.

The waiting lists reveal quite a bit about how the Canadian system has adapted to the unlimited demand for health care. Generally, waiting was longest in cardiology, orthopedics, and plastic (restorative) surgery. Patients in Newfoundland needing cardiac surgery wait an average of 42.6 weeks, an experience matched only by the 37-week average wait for plastic (restorative) surgery in Newfoundland. Waiting lists were, on average, shortest for internal medicine, where the longest wait, in British Columbia, was just over a month. In general, the waiting times for gynecology, urology, and general surgery were short — ranging from 0.9 week to 13.2 weeks.

More Waiting

It would be helpful to know whether Canadian waiting lists are getting longer or shorter over time. Although there are no comprehensive waiting list data, we can compare a 1990 measurement for British Columbia to the 1991 estimates for that province. And the result is striking: there has been a significant decline in waiting times and, in some categories, a dramatic decline. In the case of general surgery, for example, the waiting time dropped from 23.9 weeks to four weeks. In the case of urology, from 25.6 weeks to 8.3 weeks.

The explanation for this apparently good news is not, however, all that encouraging. In 1989, there was a general strike by the nurses in British Columbia, boosting the length of waiting lists dramatically. When the strike was over, waiting lists shrank.

But they didn't necessarily return to normal. Consider the effects on cardiac surgery waiting lists, as examined in an August 1991 *Journal of the American Medical Association* article by Steven J. Katz and his colleagues. In the first quarter of 1989, 400 people were waiting for bypass surgery. The province's nurses then began a work-to-rule campaign, followed by a 17-day strike. During the strike, no bypass surgeries were performed. And even after the strike there was a shortage of critical care nurses. The result: nine months of less-than-capacity operating levels and a drop in the average number of procedures per quarter, from 600 to 400. By late 1990, when the number of operations finally returned to normal, some 800 people were waiting—twice the number before the strike.

The waiting list still hasn't returned to its previous level. Our measurements show 669 people waiting in 1991, a 67-percent increase from before the strike. Because there is no unused capacity to do cardiac surgery under ordinary circumstances, the strike permanently lengthened the waiting list. (Fortunately, this problem hasn't emerged for other surgeries, except orthopedic, suggesting that those surgeries are not as dependent on specialized nurses or equipment.)

Unequal Access

Contrary to U.S. advocates of a Canadian-style system,

173

national health insurance doesn't mean equal access to health care — or equal health. One striking difference is from province to province. A woman in Newfoundland might wait 36.2 weeks for restorative surgery after a radical mastectomy, while she would wait only 13.2 weeks in the more affluent province of British Columbia. For potentially life-preserving cardiac surgeries, the difference is even larger — a disparity of 32 weeks between the longest and shortest wait. And even that disparity is misleading: New Brunswick has a short waiting list because that province only recently began to offer cardiac bypass surgery at all.

A Poor Choice

So, what can we conclude from all of this measurement of health care supply and demand in Canada? The most obvious inference is that while it is true that Canada has a good health care system, that system does not contradict the general rule that governmental production of services is expensive. Canada spends less of its Gross Domestic Product (GDP) on health care, not because we have found a way to produce health care at lower unit costs, but because we have found a way to limit the total supply of services made available. We do not permit prices to play a role in allocating health care resources in Canada. Instead, we ration the supply, denying treatment to some and making others wait.

A second inference from the data is that in Canada, neither access to health care nor medical outcomes are equal. People wait longer in some provinces than in others, and some medical technology is available in some provinces but not in others. Waiting, which is the only alternative for low-income Canadians, encourages high-income Canadians to go to the United States for treatment. The clear indication is that Americans should not adopt the Canadian health care system in the mistaken belief that it will solve the problems of access and high cost.

WHAT IS EDITORIAL BIAS?

This activity may be used as an individualized study guide for students in libraries and resource centers or as a discussion catalyst in small group and classroom discussions.

The capacity to recognize an author's point of view is an essential reading skill. The skill to read with insight and understanding involves the ability to detect different kinds of opinions or bias. **Sex bias, race bias, ethnocentric bias, political bias and religious bias** *are five basic kinds of opinions expressed in editorials and all literature that attempts to persuade. They are briefly defined in the glossary below.*

Glossary of Terms for Reading Skills

Sex Bias—the expression of dislike for and/or feeling of superiority over the opposite sex or a particular sexual minority

Race Bias—the expression of dislike for and/or feeling of superiority over a racial group

Ethnocentric Bias—the expression of a belief that one's own group, race, religion, culture or nation is superior. Ethnocentric persons judge others by their own standards and values.

Political Bias—the expression of political opinions and attitudes about domestic or foreign affairs

Religious Bias — the expression of a religious belief or attitude

Guidelines

1. From the readings in this book, locate five sentences that provide examples of editorial opinion or bias.

2. Write down each of the above sentences and determine what kind of bias each sentence represents. Is it *sex bias, race bias, ethnocentric bias, political bias* or *religious bias*?

3. Make up one sentence statements that would be an example of each of the following types of bias: *sex, race, ethnocentric, political* and *religious.*

175

BIBLIOGRAPHY

Health Care Issues

Bernstein, A. Small companies are in big pain over health care. *Business Week*, Nov. 26, 1990: p. 187.

Borger, G. Small business pulls the strings. *U.S. News & World Report*, v. 112, Jan. 20, 1992: p. 26-27.

Brandt, L. E. The future of health care in the United States. *America*, v. 167, Oct. 20, 1990: p. 272.

Butler, S. M. and E. F. Haislmaier. A national health system for America. *Heritage Foundation*, publ. 1989.

Castro, J. Condition: critical. *Time*, v. 138, Nov. 25, 1991: p. 34-40.

A decision on improving health care should not come down to a choice between two extremes. *Nation's Business*, v. 80, February 1992: p. 67.

Dentzer, S. Health care gridlock. *U.S. News & World Report*, v. 112, Jan. 20, 1992: p. 22-24.

Ellis, D. Band-aids to patch up health care. *Time*, v. 139, Feb. 17, 1992: p. 20-22.

Faltermeyer, E. Let's really cure the health system. *Fortune*, v. 125, March 23, 1992: p. 46-50.

Francis, D. A radical proposal to cure health care. *Maclean's* v. 103, March 26, 1990: p. 19.

Garland, S. B. Is Medicare a terminal case? *Business Week*, Feb. 5, 1990: p. 28.

Garland, S. B. Bush's health care Rx. *Business Week*, Feb. 3, 1992: p. 26-27.

Garland, S. B. Health care? Who cares? *Business Week*, March 30, 1992: p. 37.

Health care crisis: a special section. *USA Today* (periodical), v. 120, March 1992: p. 20-28.

Health competition. *National Review*, v. 44, Mar. 2, 1992: p. 15.

Hess, J. L. The catastrophic health care fiasco. *The Nation*, v. 250, May 21, 1990: p. 698-700.

Hood, J. Political prescriptions. *Reason*, v. 23, March 1992: p. 18-22.

Joelson, J. R. National health care is fundamental for a great modern nation. *The Humanist,* v. 50, March/April 1990: p. 35-36.

Kaihla, P. Truth and consequences. *Maclean's,* v. 105, March 23, 1992: p. 17.

Kemp, F. D. Young doctors in debt. *Christianity Today,* v. 35, Nov. 11, 1991: p. 60.

Koller, C. F. The myth of no limits. *Commonweal,* v. 119, March 27, 1992: p. 9-11.

Lowther, W. In U.S. health care, insurance is not enough. *Maclean's,* v. 105, Jan. 13, 1992: p. 37.

Morganthau, T. Cutting through the gobbledygook. *Newsweek,* v. 119, Feb. 3, 1992: p. 24-25.

Reibstein, L. Physicians, cut the costs. *Newsweek,* v. 118, Dec. 23, 1991: p. 41.

Reingold, E. M. Oregon's value judgment. *Time,* v. 138, Nov. 25, 1991: p. 37.

Shapiro, J. P. No sale on medical reform. *U.S. News & World Report,* v. 112, March 9, 1992: p. 32-33.

Sigelbaum, H. C. A rational approach to national health. *USA Today* (periodical), v. 118, March 1990: p. 68-70.

Sullman, J. Market medicine. *Reason,* v. 23, March 1992: p. 23-27.

Tevis, C. Small town prescribes own health cure. *Successful Farming,* v. 90, Jan. 1992: p. 56-58.

They play, we pay. *The Nation,* v. 254, Feb. 24, 1992: p. 219-20.

Twelve ways to cut your hospital bill. *USA Today* (periodical), v. 120, Oct. 1991: p. 13.

Weinburger, C. W. Health care for all. *USA Today* (periodical), v. 149, Feb. 3, 1992: p. 35.

Wesbury, S. National health care: no foreign models. *Current,* v. 324, July/August 1990: p. 31-34.

Witkin, G. Health care fraud. *U.S. News & World Report,* v. 112, Feb. 24, 1992: p. 34-38.

Vreeland, L. N. What to do about catastrophic's repeal. *Money,* v. 19, Jan. 1990: p. 21-22.

Costs

Controlling health care costs. *USA Today* (periodical), v. 119, Oct. 1990: p. 1-2.

Costs could soar for elderly. *USA Today* (periodical), v. 120, Feb. 1992: p. 15.

Dentzer, S. America's scandalous health care: here's how to fix it. *U.S. News & World Report,* v. 108, March 12, 1990: p. 24-28.

Hairston, D. W. Cutting the high cost of health care. *Black Enterprise,* v. 21, Nov. 1990: p. 78.

Lightfoot, D. G. Meeting skyrocketing health care costs. *USA Today* (periodical), v. 118, May 1990: p. 59-60.

Luciano, L. A cure your M.D. won't like. *Money,* special issue, Fall 1990: p. 54-56.

Matthiessen, C. Bordering on collapse. *Modern Maturity,* v. 33, Oct./Nov. 1990: p. 30-32.

Merline, J. W. "Free" medical care. *Consumer's Research Magazine,* v. 73, Fall 1990: p. 38.

Rahman, F. A doctor's remedy. *Newsweek,* v. 115, April 9, 1990: p. 10.

Ethics

Arbetter, S. R. Life-and-death decisions. *Current Health 2,* v. 18, March 1992: p. 4-8.

Bouton, K. Painful decisions: the role of the medical ethicist. *The New York Times Magazine,* Aug. 5, 1990: p. 22-25.

Buckley, J. How doctors decide who shall live, who shall die. *U.S. News & World Report,* v. 108, Jan. 22, 1990: p. 50-58.

The health care crisis. *America,* v. 163, Oct. 20, 1990: p. 262-72.

Imber, J. B. Abortion policy and medical practice. *Society,* v. 27, July/August 1990: p. 27-34.

Johnson, G. T. Is health care spiritual? *Christianity Today,* v. 34, Sept. 10, 1990: p. 29-30.

Kippen, A. Doctored results: how drug companies bribe doctors and medical journals. *The Washington Monthly,* v. 22, Oct. 1990: p. 38-42.

Menzel, P. T. Strong medicine: the ethical rationing of health care. *Oxford University Press,* 1990: 234 p.

Phalon, R. Questions with human beings attached. *Forbes,* v. 149, March 30, 1992: p. 134+.

Pushing drugs to doctors. *Consumer Reports,* v. 57, Fall 1992: p. 87-94.

Wright, R. A. The doctor's dilemma in the 21st century. *USA Today* (periodical), v. 119, Sept. 1990: p. 53-54.

Rationing

Aaron, H. J. and W. B. Schwartz. Health care rationing. *Science,* v. 248, May 11, 1990: p. 661-5.

Aaron, H. J. and W. B. Schwartz. Rationing health care: the choice before us. *Science,* v. 247, Jan. 26, 1990: p. 418-22.

Beck, M. Not enough for all. *Newsweek,* v. 115, May 14, 1991: p. 53+.

Callahan, D. Setting limits: medical goals in an aging society. Simon & Schuster, New York, 1987.

Relman, A. Don't ration health care. *Consumer's Research Magazine,* v. 73, Dec. 1990: p. 28-29.

Rothman, D. J. Rationing life. *The New York Review of Books,* v. 39, March 5, 1992: p. 32-37.

GLOSSARY

Acquired Immune Deficiency Syndrome (AIDS)

Americans for Generational Equity (AGE)

American Medical Association (AMA)

Association of Minority Health Professions School (AMHPS)

Blue Cross Blue Shield Association (BCBSA)

A computerized x-ray tube (CATscan)

Children's Defense Fund (CDF)

Catholic Health Association (CHA)

Diagnostic and Therapeutic Technology (DATTA) Assessment program

Doctor of Dental Science (DDS)

U.S. Food and Drug Administration (FDA)

Federal Poverty Line (FPL)

Federal Trade Commission (FTC)

Gross National Product (GNP)

Health Care Financing Administration (HCFA)

Human Immunodeficiency Virus (HIV)

Health Maintenance Organization (HMO)

Journal of the American Medical Association (JAMA)

Licensed Practical Nurse (LPN)

Medical Doctor (MD)

National Health Act (Canada) (NHA)

National Institute of Health (NIH)

National Restaurant Association (NRA)

Political Action Committee (PAC)

Pharmaceutical Manufacturing Association (PMA)

Resource Based Relative Value Scale (RBRVS)

Research and Development (R&D)

Registered Nurse (RN)

State Health Insurance Program (Hawaii) (SHIP)

World Health Organization (WHO)